BOOK 1 OF THE POLYAGONY TRILOGY

POLYAGONY

THE ART OF REPAIR IN OPEN RELATIONSHIPS

THE FOUNDATION

HOW TO OPEN YOUR RELATIONSHIP WITHOUT DESTROYING IT

CANDACE KLEIN

POLYAGONY, *The Foundation: How to open your relationship without destroying it* (Book One of the **Polyagony Trilogy**: The art of repair in open relationships)

VITALITY buzz, bliss + books LLC publishes original creations to grow the mission of VITALITY Cincinnati Inc, a 501(c)3 education-based nonprofit: sharing holistic self-care from neighborhood to neighborhood, person to person, and breath by breath since 2010.

Candace is grateful to Julie Maguire for creating the front cover and to Gareth Redfern Shaw and Adam Wayne for their expert editing. VITALITY is grateful Julie Lucas of withinwonder.com assists with all of VITALITY buzz, bliss + books' designs.

We invite you to honor your mind, your body, your whole self. Do only what you know to be right for you. While the invitations offered here in this book, on our websites and social media, and in our classes are geared to be gentle and easily modified by the participant to fit the participants' needs, please consult your medical doctor or health professional before undertaking any practices.

ISBN: 978-1-954688-49-0

Acknowledgements

This book was not written alone.

To my family—Andrew and Ivar—thank you for holding me through every expansion, every question, every becoming. Your love has made all of this possible.

To my partners—Adam and Katy—thank you for walking this wild, tender, complicated path with me. For your courage, your openness, and your unwavering love. This journey is richer because of you.

And to the 100 individuals and families who shared their stories—thank you for your vulnerability and trust. You are the heartbeat of this work, and part of a much larger unfolding.

This is ours.

With love,

Candace

A Note on This Series

This book is the first of three volumes.

Polyagony: The Foundation is about preparing without destroying your existing relationship — knowing yourself, building agreements with your partner, and deciding how you'll exist in the world. This is where everyone begins.

In *Polyagony: The Expansion*, we'll explore what happens when others enter — the joys and challenges of being a hinge, navigating metamour relationships, group dynamics, and play parties. That book is for when you're ready to add complexity.

In *Polyagony: The Reckoning*, we'll face the hardest parts — when things erode, when agreements break, when relationships need to end or evolve. That book is there when you need it.

But none of that matters if you don't build the foundation first.

That's what this book is for.

**In gratitude
to these friends
who pre-ordered the series as VATRONS**

Susanne Angelow, Amy Antonellis, Bonnie Arzuaga, Myra Aviles, Don Bailey, Erikaa Briones, Cosmo Buffalo, Kathryn Cascella, Matthew Cearley, Swati Chandra, Morlene Chin, Luis Chiriboga, Courtney Compton, Jim Conrad, Amber Dagit, Matty Davey, Shannon Esparza, Stephanie Fels, Kimberly Forsyth, Sarah Foster, Kara Giovannelli, Kris Girrell, Alex Goryachev, Craig Guild, Evan Hackel, Jonathan Harris, Michelle Hayward, Samantha Hoffman, Dean Huston, Tomoko Ide, Vanessa Iten, Jamie Jackson, Eric Karpinski, Carol Kell, Kyle Kitzmiller, Adam Klein, Daniel Laggner, Liz Lazar-Johnson, Vince LoRusso, Laurel Lozzi, Sheela Mahdavi, Denis Malyshev, Milena Marinkovic, Nick McKinney, Kati Moch, Chase Mower, Nataly Mower, Robert Neel, Katherine Nickerson, Gillian Norton, Michael Oirech, James Partin, Jyl Porch, Krista Powers, Evette Randolph, Gareth Redfern-Shaw, Ian Reilly, Rachel Rickards, Meredith Roberts, Marcus Rowsell, Anna Samovol, Julia Senders, Brian Shircliff, Philip Sjogren, Ryan Sweeney, Spencer Takata, Kathryn Titi, Adam Wayne, Tim Wells, Jennifer Wesley, Trish White

CONTENTS

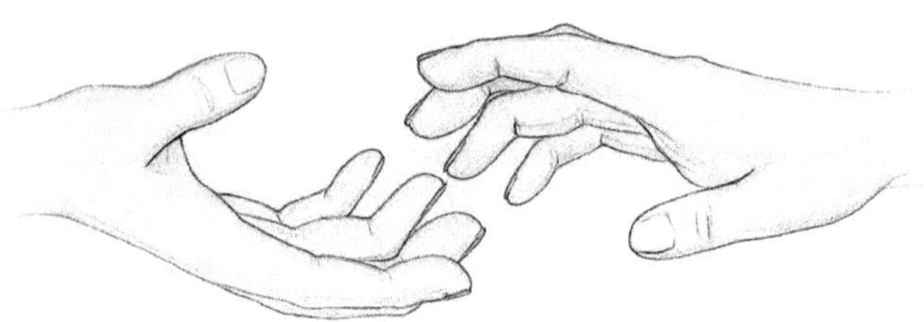

Foreword

Welcome. If you've picked up this book, chances are you're curious about open relationships. You may have considered cheating or leaving the confines of your current relationship. Maybe you've already stumbled face-first into a second relationship and are wondering what on earth just happened. Or perhaps you've been doing this for years but still find yourself tangled in unexpected emotions and complicated dynamics. Whatever brought you here, you're in the right place — and you're definitely not the only one trying to make sense of this beautiful, bewildering way of loving.

This trilogy isn't a manifesto, and it's certainly not a guide to getting polyamory "right" (spoiler: no one does). What you'll find here is a collection of hard-earned lessons, cringeworthy mistakes, tender repairs, and stories that are funny only in hindsight. Some of our experiments went beautifully; others went about as well as trying to eat soup with a fork while blindfolded and emotionally compromised. Through it all, we learned — often the hard way — what it means to love more than one person without losing ourselves in the process.

To ground this book in real experience, I interviewed 100 people who identify as "open." They ranged from long-married parents quietly navigating emotional landmines to twenty-somethings learning how to be honest for the first time. Some had been poly for decades; others were only a few awkward dates into their first attempt. Hearing their stories — their joys, their heartbreaks, their global disasters and tiny triumphs — reminded me that open relating isn't a niche hobby. It's a shared human experiment, and this book reflects the collective wisdom of those willing to speak honestly about it.

As I write this, I'm still catching my breath from my own relationship whirlwind, the kind that rearranges your inner furniture without asking permission. It began when I unexpectedly fell for someone new. Suddenly I found myself on jet-set weekends full of passion, late-night conversations, and the kind of dizzying excitement that makes you forget to eat. It was intoxicating, beautiful... and far more complicated than I wanted to admit.

And, like most open relationships, the fantasy didn't survive contact with reality. Alongside the romance came heartbreak, insecurity, confusion, and several moments where I questioned my own sanity. Love may be abundant, but time and emotional bandwidth is not, a truth I learned the hard way. If anything, these chaotic, beautiful, painful experiences became the clearest motivation to write this book: not from theory, but from lived, messy truth.

I share these raw experiences not to sensationalize them, but because they reveal the real terrain of open relating, the tenderness, the missteps, the unexpected grief and joy. There's a reason this trilogy is called **Polyagony**: it's not just about the beauty of loving many, but the very human chaos that comes with it.

Open relating — whether it's polyamory, swinging, ethical

non-monogamy, or relationship anarchy — comes in a thousand flavors. It's gloriously human and often gloriously messy. It reveals sharp edges we didn't know we had, and sometimes we only notice them when we're already bleeding. Most books skip the part where people fall flat on their faces; I didn't want to. ***Polyagony*** is about the paper cuts, the spirals, the jealousy spikes, the unexpected grief, the "oh god, I thought I was fine with that" moments. If you can see some of the pitfalls before you fall into them — or at least laugh when you're already knee-deep — that's half the battle.

When I began writing Polyagony, I realized how much of the conversation around open relating focuses on ideals rather than reality. We hear about compersion, freedom, and endless possibility, far less about confusion, insecurity, misunderstandings, or the logistical chaos of multiple relationships. There are wonderful books and therapists out there, but the gritty, vulnerable, "please tell me I'm not the only one who has messed this up" conversations are still rare. This trilogy aims to fill that gap.

That's where I come in. After more than a decade of open relating — with relationships that ranged from life-changing to "what on earth was I thinking?" — I've gathered enough stories and lessons to fill several books. I approach all of this with a light heart, because if we can't occasionally laugh at our own romantic disasters, we won't survive the rest of the journey.

If you choose to walk this path, you will screw up, repeatedly. That's not a failure of character; it's part of the curriculum. Every relationship style has its challenges, but open relating has a way of amplifying whatever you've been avoiding. What will keep you grounded isn't perfection, but a commitment to your values, honesty, communication and a sense of humor. We're all experimenting with love using the tools we have, and sometimes those tools are a little blunt.

Not long ago, my friend and former co-author Kris — a clinical psychologist and one of the wisest people I know — gave me a perspective that stayed with me. When I told him I was writing this book, he smiled and said, "Well, I'm polyamorous. Aren't we all? My love didn't shrink when I had more children; it expanded." His words hit a nerve in the best way. Love isn't a finite resource. This book takes that truth seriously, offering insights not just for those opening their relationships, but for anyone learning how to let their heart grow without losing themselves.

So take a breath. Grab a notebook. Maybe a drink. Join me as I explore the triumphs, train wrecks, and tender truths of open relating. You're not alone in the agony, and you're certainly not alone in the joy. We're in this together — learning, stumbling, laughing, and growing our way through the beautifully complex tapestry of love.

Welcome to the adventure.

Polyamory invites a whole new language. For a helpful list of definitions and much more, visit my website:

www.polyagony.com

Introduction:
The Beautiful Mess

Polyamory isn't about being right or wrong. What this book offers is something rarer: an honest look at the messy middle, the cringeworthy mistakes, the painful crashes, the surprising joys, and the small repairs that make open relating not just possible, but deeply worthwhile. This isn't theory. It's lived experience.

I've been there, and I've been both brilliant at this and terrible at this. I've cried, laughed, broken things, fixed them, and learned more about myself in the process than I ever thought possible. In Polyagony, there is compersion, love, connection and intimacy, and there's also jealousy, scheduling disasters, awkward conversations, and the humbling realization that you're not nearly as enlightened as you hoped. Polyamory has a special talent for showing you the parts of yourself you've been avoiding. Let's start with a few moments that broke me—and people like me—wide open. What follows is a taste of what you can expect in this series, the early cracks where the light and the learning first slip through.

The Crying in the Bedroom and the Silent Consent

"I thought I was ready. We'd had the talks, we'd read the books, we'd promised each other we were solid. I thought

I'd done my work. I mean, I had been doing this for years, so I was clearly ready.

And then one night, my partner and I had a threesome with a good friend of mine. I wanted to be happy for us, I really did. But instead I felt like the ground beneath me disappeared. I couldn't breathe. As they cuddled, glowing and content on the living room sofa, I sat on the edge of my bed sobbing, chest tight, wondering why the hell I had ever initiated any of it. For a moment, I was convinced that I had lost them both.

I hated that part of myself. I wanted to be the evolved, loving partner who celebrated my partner's joy. Instead, I was unraveling. That was the night I realized polyamory wasn't going to just stretch me. It was going to pull me apart in ways I'd need to consciously stitch back together."

Polyamory will drag your shadows into the light. You'll discover jealousy you thought you'd outgrown. You'll realize your "I'm fine" was a lie. And you'll learn—sometimes painfully—that honesty matters more than harmony.

NRE: Ecstasy and Burnout

"When I first felt NRE—new relationship energy—I thought I was floating. I couldn't stop smiling. Food tasted better, music sounded richer. The whole world felt brighter. I wanted to freeze the feeling and live inside it.

But NRE doesn't only make you feel high. It makes you reckless. I ignored red flags, I made impossible promises, I convinced myself that love alone could override logistics and emotional reality. It couldn't. The crash was brutal. I found myself trying to repair relationships I had neglected in the glow of a new one, and in some cases the damage was already done."

NRE can be thrilling, transformative, inspiring. It can also burn your relationships down if you treat it as truth rather than chemistry. The goal isn't to suppress it, but rather enjoy it while keeping some part of yourself tethered to reality.

The Awkward Honesty of Testing

"One of my most awkward moments wasn't about jealousy. It was about health. I remember sitting with a new potential partner, trying to bring up STI testing. My throat tightened. My heart raced. I was terrified that if I shared my HSV status, they would walk away. For all my talk of openness, I suddenly felt sixteen again, fumbling through a conversation I wasn't sure I knew how to have.

They were kind. They asked thoughtful questions. They held my hand. We talked about boundaries, testing rhythms, safety plans. It wasn't glamorous. But it was intimate in a way that surprised me. They saw me clearly and didn't flinch."
Open relationships demand conversations many people never have. About sex. About risk. About jealousy. About safety. About livelihoods and kids and emotional bandwidth. These conversations are tender, uncomfortable, sometimes funny, and absolutely necessary.

Over-Talking and Not Listening

"There was a time we had what one of us thought was a perfectly clear agreement—until it wasn't. We ended up in a circular, exhausting conversation where both of us pushed harder and listened less. Every sentence felt like a counterargument rather than a bridge. By the end, we weren't closer. We were just tired.

That was when it hit me that communication isn't about saying all the right things. It's about hearing the things you don't want to."

Over-talking is one of the most common problems in open relating. We think communication will save us, and it can, but only if it includes listening. Otherwise we're just competing monologues.

The Arc of This Trilogy

So what do we do with all these stories, the crying in the bedroom, the silent consent, the NRE highs and lows, the awkward honesty, the miscommunications. We use them as maps. As warnings. As invitations to do better, not perfectly, but better.

Here's what's ahead:

In *Polyagony: The Foundation*:

- **So You Want to Be Poly?** Getting clear on why you want this, and what you've absorbed from culture that might not serve you.

- **Defining Your Poly.** Exploring your own terms, communication style, desires, and identity so you don't end up living someone else's script.

- **Un-monogamize Yourself–Interacting with Partners.**
  Forming agreements, exploring hopes and fears, and
  establishing a cadence for communication with your
  partner.

- **Your Place in this World.** Whether single or coupled,
  a parent or not, understand who else will be impacted
  when you open up.

In *Polyagony: The Expansion*:

- **Getting Into Action.** Moving from theory into practice,
  navigating discomfort, first dates, metamours,
  awkward feelings, and the emotional turbulence of
  early open relating.

- **Group Play Dynamics.** The protocols, insecurities,
  surprises, and joys of group intimacy.

- **I'm coming out.** How to decide when and with
  whom to disclose.

In *Polyagony: The Reckoning*:

- **Death by a Thousand Papercuts.** The everyday
  mess of open relating: NRE, jealousy, pacing
  mismatches, broken agreements.

- **Deal Breakers.** The hard lines: safety, honesty,
  integrity, and what happens when trust fractures.

- **Relationship Evolution and Individuation.** How to
  stay connected without losing yourself, and how to
  love others without abandoning your core.

- **Breakups.** De-escalation, grief, polycule fallout, and how to end relationships without destroying the whole ecosystem.

Your Turn

Before you dive into *Polyagony: The Foundation*, take a moment with yourself:

▶ What drew you to this book? Curiosity? Crisis? Desire? Fear?

▶ What do you imagine open relating will give you? What do you worry it might take away?

▶ What rule or expectation about relationships have you absorbed that might not survive contact with polyamory?

▶ When you picture yourself at your most jealous, what do you tend to do? What do you wish you could do instead?

Write your answers down, or just think them through. You're not trying to impress anyone. You're trying to understand yourself. This book won't tell you how to be perfect. It will offer real stories from real people who learned how to survive the agonies long enough to reach the beauty on the other side.

You will cry. You will laugh. You will mess up. You will grow. That is the nature of open relating.

So take a breath. Grab your notebook. Join us. You're not alone in this mess.

Part One:

Preparing Yourself

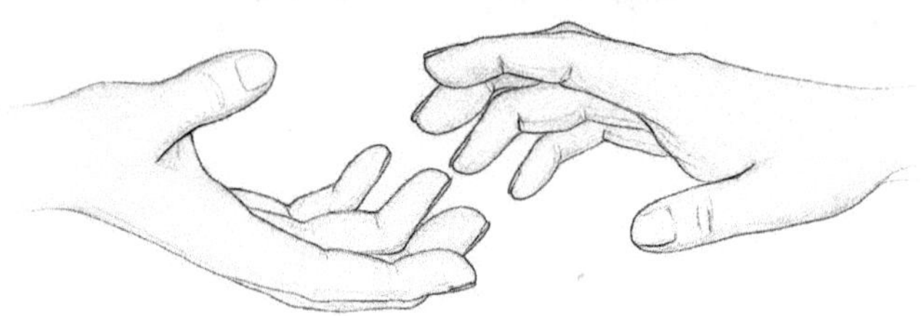

Chapter 1
So you want to be poly - are you sure?

"A world where it is safe to love
is a world where it is safe to live."

Anderlini-D'Onofrio, 2004

If you're reading this, there's a good chance something about monogamy isn't working the way you hoped it would. Maybe you've cheated. Maybe you've thought about it. Maybe you just feel restless, curious, or trapped between wanting more and not wanting to hurt the person you love. Maybe you have walked away from a relationship and are looking for a new way.

This chapter is where we slow down. Before you open anything, before you download an app, before you swipe right, or buy a ticket to a play party, we need to talk about why you're here in the first place.

Before you open your relationship, pause for a moment. Ask yourself one honest question: Why am I doing this?

It sounds simple, but this is the point where most relationships begin to wobble. If you're not clear on your motivation, you're not just taking a risk. You're walking in blind. And that's how relationships quietly start to unravel after opening. Sooner or later, you'll trip over something you never saw coming.

▲ Fuck Up: I don't know why I'm poly

When asked why she chose to become polyamorous, Cindy froze. She wasn't confused, she wasn't conflicted — she simply had no answer. Her partner had been nudging her toward polyamory for years, sending articles, podcasts, and the occasional "we should talk about this someday" text. She loved him, she trusted him, and she genuinely wanted to be supportive. So she said yes.

But when pressed for her own "why", she realized she didn't have one. Not a personal one. Not a lived one. And without a true why of her own, the path she followed wasn't really hers. Five years later, married with a child, she found herself in a relationship that didn't feel like hers. She was trying to balance what she needed with what her partner hoped their polyamory would become, and instead of expanding, her life felt smaller. She wasn't broken. She was simply stuck living someone else's why.

Why is polyamory appealing to YOU? Is it because you are struggling in a relationship and want to give yourself some latitude? Are you drawn to a new way of living? Or perhaps you're in love with someone else and trying to reconcile that love within your existing primary relationship? Do you have a high sex drive and need more outlets? Or are you having trouble seeing yourself in an intimate and loving relationship with only one person? Establishing clarity around your "why" is essential.

You don't need a psychology degree to know this. If you aren't clear on why you're opening your relationship, you're far more likely to end up in "Cindy trouble." Maybe you're not actually drawn to polyamory. Maybe you're doing it because your partner wants it. In that case, the whole arrangement will feel as comfortable as wearing your mom's prom dress to the grocery store. Technically possible, but deeply wrong for you.

Your motivation doesn't have to impress anyone, but it does need to be your own.

▲ Fuck Up: I want out, so I'll be poly

Sully and Jen didn't sit down one night with a glass of wine and a sense of adventure thinking, "Let's open our marriage." Their story started on a Tuesday, because of course it did, the day when nothing good ever happens. Jen found the messages. Not flirty messages. Not ambiguous messages. The kind of messages that make your stomach drop.

Sully cried. Jen yelled. They did the familiar dance couples do when betrayal enters the room:

"I'm sorry." "How could you?" "I'll fix it." "Fix what?" "Us." They slept in separate rooms for a week. He brought flowers. She threw the flowers away. He sent long paragraphs beginning with "I never meant to hurt you" and ending with "please don't give up on us."

Then, one night, exhausted from circling the same pain, Jen suggested opening the marriage.

"I just don't want to feel blindsided again," she said quietly. "If you're going to feel things for other people, I want it to be honest."

It sounded brave. It sounded progressive. It sounded like something a relationship podcast host would applaud. But the problem wasn't polyamory. It was the wound underneath.

Whenever Sully started to connect with someone new, Jen felt the betrayal all over again. A woman from his hiking group. Someone he met at a friend's party. It didn't matter who. The ache returned. She'd get triggered, lash out, bring up the cheating in front of new partners, or cancel her own plans at the last minute because she was spiraling. Their "open marriage" was really just the original hurt reenacted with new people caught in the splash zone.

And Sully believed that because he was being honest now, his past mistake had somehow been erased. But honesty and healing aren't the same thing.

They weren't moving toward something they wanted. They were running from something they couldn't face.
Jen wasn't choosing polyamory. She was choosing a survival strategy.

Sully wasn't choosing expansion. He was choosing atonement.

It's hard to make good decisions when you're still bleeding. The truth is simple; you can't build a new way of loving if your only motivation is to escape the old one. Polyamory works best when you're moving toward something you genuinely want, not scrambling away from something you fear. Opening from pain almost always leads to more pain. Opening from clarity and choice gives you a fighting chance.

♥ Exercise: 7 Levels of Why

If you'd like to see the 7 levels of why applied to real-life relationship examples, please visit

www.polyagony.com/7levelsofwhy.

Grab a notebook and answer these questions as honestly as you can:

▶ What excites you about open relationships?

▶ What scares you about them?

▶ Do you see this as part of who you are, or something you're curious to explore?

▶ How do you want your partner, or partners, to see it? What would hurt more: giving this up, or never trying at all?

These questions aren't meant to overwhelm you; they're warming you up for the harder part, which is getting underneath your first answer. Most people stop at the surface. "I want more excitement." "I want more intimacy." "I want more freedom." Those are beginnings. They aren't the truth yet.

Now we dig.

Choose one of your answers — any one that feels charged, interesting, or uncomfortable — and ask yourself: Why is that important to me?

Whatever answer you write next, ask the same question again. And again. And again. Seven times total.

It will feel repetitive, but that's the point. The first two or three answers tend to be social answers. The ones you could tell a friend without breaking a sweat. By the fifth or sixth "why", you're usually closer to the fear you've been hiding or the desire you haven't yet said out loud.

Here's an example.

Let's say your first answer is:
   "I want more excitement and variety."

Why?
   "Because I feel something is missing."

Why does that matter?
   "Because I'm scared life is passing me by."

Why does that matter?
   "Because I've spent years putting my needs second."

Why?
   "Because I didn't feel like I was allowed to want more."

And so on.

You don't need polished answers. You don't need perfect sentences. You only need honesty and enough curiosity to keep going until something real shows up on the page.

My friend Kris Girrell (mentioned in the Foreword) taught me this. He says it usually takes seven rounds to get to the real driver, the one sitting underneath the excuses, the fear, and the performance. Most people never get that far, which is why they end up making choices that don't match what they actually need.

Being poly doesn't make you enlightened, edgy, or better at love. Knowing why you're doing this — your why, not someone else's — is what determines whether this path becomes sustainable or blows up in your hands.

What do you want?

"I'll tell you what I want, what I really really want"

Spice Girls, 1996

Most of us can list everything we don't want without breaking a sweat. But ask, "What do you actually want?" and suddenly the room gets uncomfortably quiet. Desire is simple in theory and annoyingly complex in real life. It shifts with time, with partners, with emotion, with season. And yet this question matters more than almost anything else in open relating. Without a vision for your life — not a perfect one, just an honest one — you'll drift. You'll end up reacting to other people's choices instead of making your own.

For five years, I taught emotional intelligence work in a leadership academy. If there's one thing I learned, it's that action without vision is just busywork. You can fill your schedule and still feel empty. On the flip side, vision without action is nothing more than fantasy. To build relationships that feel aligned and nourishing, you need both. And that starts with naming what you want, even if that truth feels clumsy or inconvenient.

▲ Fuck Up: I don't know what I want, but I don't want this

Jack had a talent for talking about everything that wasn't working in his love life. When we met, he launched into a detailed monologue about how his partners never made him feel special, never put in enough effort, never remembered his boundaries, never asked the right questions, never "showed up." He spoke for nearly an hour without taking a breath. It was impressive in its own way.

When he finally paused, I asked a simple question.

"Okay. Instead of listing what you don't want, tell me what you do want."

Jack blinked at me, confused. "I just told you."

He hadn't. He'd given me a catalogue of disappointments, but not a single desire. Jack believed he'd communicated his needs, but what he had actually done was narrate his pain. He'd never taken the time to clarify what feeling valued, considered, or "special" would look like in practice. He expected his partners to guess his internal landscape, then felt abandoned when they guessed wrong.

This is one of the most common pitfalls in open relating. If you don't know what you want, no one else will be able to meet you there. And if you're not willing to name your desires out loud, your relationships will devolve into misunderstandings, mismatched expectations, and disappointment disguised as resentment.

Clarity doesn't guarantee you'll get what you want. But lack of clarity almost guarantees you won't.

♥ Exercise: The Perfect Day

To listen to a recorded meditation of The Perfect Day, visit www.polyagony.com/theperfectday.

If you're struggling to name what you want — really want — here's a way in. Not through logic, but through imagination. Close your eyes for a moment and picture waking up on a day five years from now. Not a fantasy day filled with yachts and champagne, just a day where your life feels aligned.

Where do you wake up? What do you see outside your window? Who, if anyone, is beside you? A long-term partner? A lover? Your child? Your cat? Yourself in the mirror?

What does the morning feel like? Are you moving slowly or with energy? Do you make breakfast with someone? Sit in the sun? What tone opens the day?

Walk yourself through it with curiosity.

How do you spend your afternoon? Who do you spend time

with? Do you feel grounded? Creative? Adventurous? Rested?

And when the day comes to an end, what does "coming home" look like? Warmth? Quiet? Playfulness? A house filled with multiple partners and kids? A small apartment just for you? What feels safe to your body? What feels alive?

You're not building a five-year plan. You're listening for emotional resonance. Write down anything that stood out — images, feelings, pacing, who was there, who wasn't. Your nervous system will often tell the truth long before your conscious mind does.

As you reflect, consider two areas:

Your personal life. Are you healthy, rested, energized, or fulfilled?

Your relational life. Are you in multiple connections? One deep one? Renewing a long-term bond? Exploring something new?

Let this vision inform you. It's a starting point.

What is your truest desire?

> "The fastest way to change your life
> is to change your focus."

Tony Robbins, 2014

▲ Fuck Up: I'm in flow

When I first moved to San Diego, I met an entire subset of people who believed they could manifest their way through any situation. They talked about being "in flow" the way some people talk about being gluten-free. One of them was Maria. She was magnetic, charismatic, surrounded by friends, and always in the middle of some fascinating short-term romance. She also hadn't paid a bill on time in three years, felt chronically unfulfilled, and changed life paths every six weeks.

Maria wanted depth, purpose, connection, and stability, but she refused to name what any of those things looked like. When I asked her for one specific goal she could focus her energy on, she smiled serenely and said, "I don't want to premeditate life. I'm in flow."

That's when I realized something important. "Flow" without direction is just drifting. You can feel spiritual and inspired and still be stuck. You can have chemistry with twelve people in a year and still feel lonely. You can spend hours dreaming and never take one step toward a life that feels good in practice.

Maria wasn't doing anything wrong. She simply hadn't learned that intuition and intention work best when they work together.

♥ Exercise: Creating Your Dream List

To see a detailed description and interactive dream list tool, please visit www.polyagony.com/dreamlist.

To avoid Maria's fate, it helps to get concrete. One of the most effective tools I've found is creating a "Dream List", adapted from Matthew Kelly's book *The Dream Manager*. Think of it as a way to understand what your heart is reaching for, not what you think you're supposed to want.

Start by imagining what you want across different areas of your life. Maybe you dream of having a partner you can cry with, someone who can hold you without flinching. Or maybe you want a lover who takes you on wild adventures and pushes you to take risks you'd never take on your own. Maybe you want a peaceful home, a community of friends, or a relationship that lets you breathe.

Write every dream down. Big ones, small ones, ridiculous ones. Don't edit yourself.

Categorize Your Dreams: Create a page with columns including: Sexuality, Romance, Family, Finances, Intimacy, Communication, Adventure and Risk. Add others if you want; this is your life.

Time Frames: Under each category, write three sections marked: six months, five years, and lifetime. This helps you see what's urgent, what's developing, and what's part of your long-term heart.

Dream Big: Aim for at least 25 dreams. More if you can.

Let yourself want things without apologizing for the size of them.

Identify Support: Next to each dream, write the name of someone who could support that dream coming alive. It could be a partner, a lover, a friend, a mentor, or even someone you haven't met yet. This isn't about assigning responsibility; it's about recognizing who already aligns with your desires.

Communicate: When it feels right, tell the people you listed. Let them know how they fit into the life you're building, even in small ways. It strengthens connection and clarity.

Find Your Truest Desire: Finally, look at each category and circle the dream that resonates most right now. Not the most impressive dream. Not the most convenient. The one that makes your body lean forward. Do this for each timeframe so patterns can emerge.

♥ *The Dream List on the next page might help!*

DREAM LIST	6 months	5 years	lifetime
Example	*Meet my life partner (Mom)*	*Have my first child (Bestie Krista)*	*Take my family around the world for a year (Sister Jane)*
Spirituality			
Family			
Sexuality/Romance			
Intimacy			
Finances			
Communication			
Adventure			
Risk			

You'll start to see themes. You'll see where your heart keeps pointing. That clarity will help you build relationships and choices that match the life you actually want, not the one you think you should settle for.

Embarking on polyamory takes more than curiosity or the desire for new experiences. It asks you to look inward with honesty, to question your motives, and to build a vision that reflects who you are rather than who you're trying to please. Understanding your "why" isn't a box-checking exercise. It's the foundation for every choice you'll make from here on out.

Whether you're drawn to polyamory because of sex, love, adventure, personal growth, self-discovery, or something you've never quite had the words for, the important thing is to pause long enough to understand yourself. When you act from clarity rather than confusion, you make choices that support your relationships instead of slowly eroding them. The exercises in this chapter aren't magic spells, but they've helped many people navigate the emotional chaos that often accompanies open relating. They give you something solid to hold onto when everything else feels uncertain. They help you avoid the quiet build-up of resentment, miscommunication, and disappointment that can sneak into even the most loving relationships.

Before you talk about open relationships with anyone else, sit with your answers. Let them be honest, messy, or incomplete. Then, when you're ready, bring that truth into a conversation with your partner.

Not to convince them.

Not to negotiate.

But to be honest about where you are and what you're feeling.

Opening a relationship doesn't start with new lovers. It starts with a real conversation with your current partner.

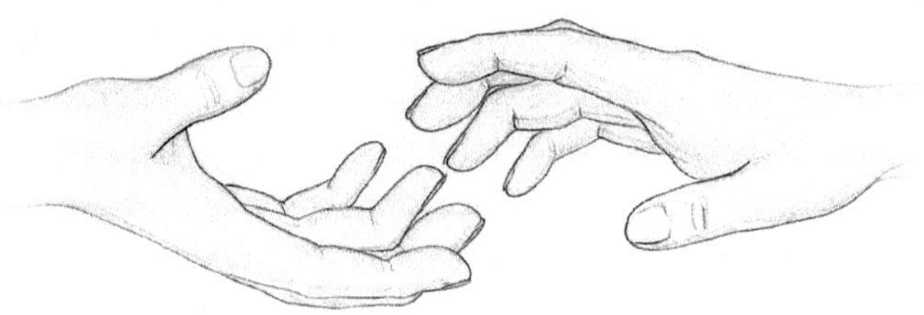

Chapter 2
Defining Your Poly

"What would you say you do here?"

Bob Slydell, *Office Space*

▲ Fuck Up: I don't want to ruin the vibe by talking about it

Chris and Anna were the kind of couple people noticed the moment they walked into a room. Attractive, warm, mid-30s, the type who seemed effortlessly social. They were also dating other people, both together and separately. When new partners asked how they identified or what they were looking for, they'd smile and say, "We're just having fun." If anyone pushed for clarity, they waved it off. "Let's keep it light." They weren't actually keeping anything simple.

The problem was that Chris and Anna weren't actually keeping anything light. Their laissez-faire approach left a trail of strained and confusing connections. They ghosted after dates because they didn't want uncomfortable conversations. They avoided certain events because they didn't want to bump into someone they'd casually abandoned. In their local community, they slowly developed a reputation as a couple who used people for sex and disappeared when emotions got real.

This pattern is incredibly common in early non-monogamy. When you don't define yourself or your intentions, other people fill in the blanks, and they rarely assume the best. The non-monogamy community is still relatively small, and word travels fast. You don't need a five-page relationship manifesto, but you do need enough clarity to help others understand what to expect from you.

Some definitions are helpful. Knowing how you identify, what you're open to, how you prefer to relate, and how you communicate gives potential partners something to stand on. It helps you understand yourself, and it offers the person across from you a shared language. The terminology around polyamory can get complicated, but this chapter offers a simple starting point. It won't cover everything — that would take a new Webster's — but it will give you a solid starting point for clearer conversations and fewer unintentional heartbreaks.

Identity vs. Lifestyle

"You are what you believe yourself to be."

Paulo Coelho, *The Alchemist*

Polyamory means very different things to different people. For some, it feels like an orientation — it's their identity, something woven into who they are. For others, it feels like a lifestyle, a choice they make because it fits a particular season of their life. Neither path is wrong; what matters is knowing which one feels true for you, and understanding that your answer might shift as you evolve.

How do I know if polyamory is an Identity for me?

For a lot of people, it starts with a moment. A sentence. A realization so clear it almost makes your stomach drop. Something inside you says, "I can't do monogamy anymore," and even if you don't fully understand it yet, you know it's true.

For me, the signs were there far earlier. I cheated on every partner I ever had in my twenties. Fidelity wasn't just hard; it was something I couldn't sustain, no matter how much guilt followed. At twenty, with my first serious partner, I already knew I didn't want to be confined to one relationship. I got engaged young, panicked, and ended it just as quickly. The engagement wasn't the problem. The expectation of monogamy was. It felt like I was being squeezed into a life that didn't fit, so I threw myself into a promiscuous lifestyle the moment I began having sex.

But here's the part that matters: I wasn't unethical because I didn't care about people. I was unethical because I didn't yet have a framework that let me be honest. I was always polyamorous, I just didn't know how to be ethical about it until much later.

Many people who later identify as polyamorous share a similar pattern. It's not always about wanting endless partners. Sometimes it's about the discomfort of pretending you only have room in your heart for one person when that hasn't been your experience.

The important distinction is this: identity doesn't excuse harm. It simply helps you understand the kind of structure you need in order to live honestly.

▲ Fuck Up: I'm not poly anymore

After several years of open marriage, Faith became convinced that her husband, Wayne, wasn't really interested in polyamory anymore. He never said as much, but she took every hesitation, every insecurity, and every uncomfortable moment as evidence. So she made what she thought was the loving choice: she decided she would become monogamous. Faith reached out to all of her lovers and told them she was "switching over," stepping back from poly to support her marriage. They were gracious. They understood. They reassured her. And she marched herself into monogamy with the enthusiasm of someone doing something noble and self-sacrificing.

The problem was that Wayne never asked for any of this. He didn't ask her to shut down connections. He didn't want her to contort herself into a version that never really existed. Faith didn't realize how much of herself she'd amputated until the resentment started to creep in. She became irritable, withdrawn, and oddly hollow. Eventually Wayne looked at her and said, "Enough. I didn't ask you to give this up, and I don't want you resenting me for something I never even wanted."

And he was right.

So Faith reached out to her lovers again, apologized, and returned to herself — the actual self, not the version she tried to force into place.

The fuck up wasn't choosing monogamy or polyamory. The fuck up was pretending to hold one worldview while secretly hoping for another.

Lifestyle Polyamory

For other people, polyamory doesn't feel like an identity at all. It feels like a choice. Maybe they're curious. Maybe they're in a phase of life where exploration feels exciting and appropriate. Maybe they've built enough trust in their relationship that opening feels like an adventure rather than a threat.

Neither path is superior. What causes problems is when people assume everyone is coming from the same place. Someone who sees polyamory as a deep identity may feel devastated if a partner wants to "close the relationship" later. Someone who sees it as a temporary lifestyle experiment may feel trapped if their partner treats it as a permanent orientation.

Clarity about where you fall on that spectrum helps you find people who want something similar.

Give It a Name

"Words are the most powerful drug used by mankind."

Rudyard Kipling
Speech to the Royal College of Surgeons, 1923

When you don't define your structure, people fill in the blanks with their own assumptions. And those assumptions are often wrong.

If you say "We're just seeing what happens," one person might hear:

"This is casual."

"There are no rules."

"Feelings are welcome."

"Feelings are dangerous."

All at the same time.

Lack of definition doesn't create freedom. It usually creates confusion, and confusion is one of the fastest ways to hurt people unintentionally.

▲ Fuck Up: Not following protocol

Enrique and Abbey had been open for years. They were comfortable dating separately and had learned most of their lessons the slow way. At an event, they met Sasha and Penny, a couple with amazing chemistry. They flirted, connected, and left the night excited about exploring more. A few days later, Enrique texted Penny to ask her out. Hours passed. Then a day. Then two. Eventually both he and Abbey realized they were being ghosted. Weeks later, they learned why. Sasha and Penny were swingers who only played together, and Enrique's solo message violated their personal protocol. To Sasha and Penny, it wasn't a small *faux pas*; it was fundamental disrespect.

Enrique and Abbey hadn't done anything malicious. They simply hadn't clarified definitions or preferences upfront.

The result was confusion, hurt feelings, and a missed connection that could have been avoided with one honest conversation.

Open relating has a surprisingly wide vocabulary — and a shockingly high number of unspoken rules depending on the community you're in. You don't need to know everything, but it helps to know yourself well enough to communicate clearly. Which is why I created an online dictionary that I update regularly at www.polyagony.com/dictionary.

It exists exactly for moments like these, when a shared definition could have saved everyone a headache.

Key Terminology for This Chapter

Once you start exploring non-monogamy, one of the first questions people will ask is simple:

"What kind of poly are you?"

That question can feel overwhelming, especially when you're new. But you don't need to memorize a dictionary of terms. You just need enough clarity to describe how you actually live.

Here are a few broad structures people tend to use (see full dictionary at www.polyagony.com/dictionary):

Open relationship: A couple stays romantically primary, but allows outside sexual or romantic connections.

Swinging: Typically focused on sexual experiences, often shared as a couple.

Polyamory: Multiple romantic relationships with the knowledge and consent of everyone involved, but often experienced apart.

Relationship anarchy: Rejecting traditional relationship hierarchies and designing each connection individually.

These labels aren't cages. They're shortcuts for communication.

♥ **Exercise: Name Yourself**

To see a more detailed version of the naming questionnaire, visit www.polyagony.com/nameyourself.

Take a few minutes and answer these questions:

▶ Do I see polyamory as part of my identity, or as a lifestyle choice?

▶ Am I looking for sexual exploration, romantic connection, or both?

▶ Do I want a primary partner, or do I prefer non-hierarchical connections?

▶ What am I actually available for right now?

Now try to write one simple sentence that describes your current structure.

Not your ideal structure. Not your future structure. Just your honest, present-day answer.

For example:

"I'm married and exploring casual connections."

"I'm single and open to multiple romantic partners."

"I'm curious about polyamory, but still mostly monogamous in practice."

This sentence will probably change over time. That's normal. The goal isn't permanence. The goal is honesty.

Envisioning Your Ideal Poly Life

What does an ideal poly life look like for you? Not the version you think you're supposed to want, or the one that looks good on Instagram, but the version that would genuinely feel nourishing. Maybe you imagine one anchor partner and a few lighter lover connections. Maybe you want multiple deep, committed relationships that all matter in different ways. Maybe you want something that doesn't even have language yet.

Whatever the shape, it helps to name it.

▲ Fuck Up: Playing a different game

Jonny and Sarah spent years happily identifying as swingers. They liked playing together, being social, having fun. Eventually they started dating independently, and at first everything felt light and exciting. Jonny was content keeping things casual, staying emotionally unavailable, and enjoying the freedom of low-stakes encounters.

Sarah, however, met someone who changed the game for her. She started seeing one partner regularly. Feelings grew. Vulnerability crept in. She fell in love.

Jonny panicked. He told her he wasn't comfortable with her loving someone else and asked her to end it. She did, reluctantly, and the breakup devastated both her and her lover. She felt torn between her marriage and her heart. To keep the peace, she shifted to looking for just one additional casual partner outside her marriage — something more emotionally grounded.

Jonny, however, hated this new structure. He wanted everything to stay "light," which, to him, meant short-term and varied. Meanwhile, Sarah found herself over-consuming at parties just to get into the mindset Jonny preferred, pushing past her emotional limits to fit a version of poly that no longer matched who she was.

Something felt deeply off to her, and for good reason.
They weren't playing the same game anymore. One of them had changed levels; the other hadn't noticed, or hadn't wanted to.

It's impossible to predict what you'll want five years from now. Your desires will shift as you grow, connect, get hurt, fall in love, feel secure, feel insecure, raise children, change careers, move cities, meet new people, or simply evolve into a version of yourself you couldn't have imagined earlier.

That's normal.

What matters is communicating your desires as they change and giving your partners the chance to meet you where you are. Trying to force yourself into a relational structure that doesn't fit — whether it's "keep things light," "don't fall in love," "always be available," or "never catch feelings" — will eventually collapse under its own weight.

Different people can play different games in the same relationship if everyone agrees to the rules. But trying to contort yourself into something that contradicts your truth is a slow erosion of self. And no dynamic — poly, mono, hierarchical, anarchist, or anything in between — can survive that forever.

Closing Reflection

Definitions don't lock you in. They give other people a map. And they give you a mirror.

When you can say what you're doing and why, you create a foundation for trust. When you can't, you create a fog where people project their hopes, fears, and fantasies onto you.

Before you go looking for new or varied partners, take your one-sentence definition and share it with the person you're already in relationship with.

Just to say, "Here's where I am right now." That conversation is the real beginning of opening a relationship.

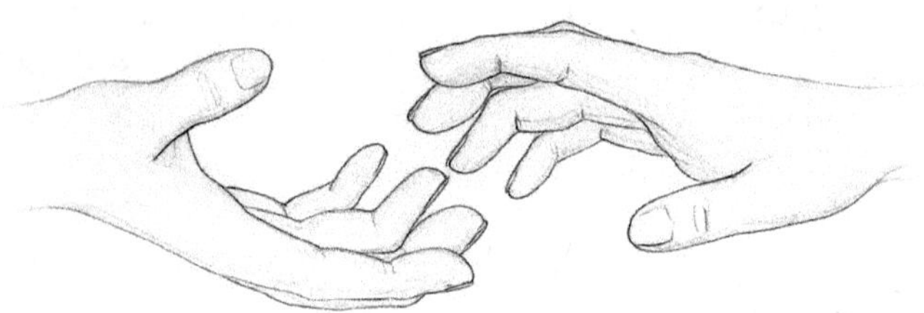

Chapter 3
Erotic Blueprint

"Tell me what a person finds sexually attractive and I
will tell you their entire philosophy of life."

Ayn Rand, *For the New Intellectual*

Understanding the way you relate, date, and emotionally
connect is important — but understanding your erotic
wiring can change the way you openly relate. Your erotic
blueprint isn't just about what arouses you. It's about how
you experience pleasure, how you give and receive erotic
energy, and how you feel safe and seen in sexual spaces.

Jaiya introduced the Erotic Blueprint system to a wider
audience through the television series Sex, Love & Goop
(2021). Since that time, it has since become one of the
most useful tools for couples and polycules to navigate
compatibility. The quiz takes about fifteen minutes, but the
insight it gives you can save months of mismatched intimacy,
misunderstandings, and avoidable heartbreak. You can find
it here: www.polyagony.com/blueprintquiz

Knowing your erotic blueprint helps you meet your own
needs. Knowing your partners' blueprints helps you meet
theirs.

▲ Fuck Up: I'm not just Down to Fuck

Lillith had one of the roughest entries into polyamory. She assumed everyone in the community approached sex with the same intentionality she did: slowly, carefully, deliberately. Instead, she kept meeting people who seemed ready to jump into bed before she'd even finished her drink. It wasn't that she was shy or prudish. She simply needed time, connection, trust. But online, at parties, and in person, people kept coming at her hot and heavy. To her, it felt disrespectful. To them, it was normal.

She started wondering, "Is there even a place for me here? If I'm not someone who fucks right away, am I doing poly wrong?"

Of course not. Poly doesn't mean slutty. Poly doesn't mean you have to be sexually available on demand.

Lillith wasn't an outsider. She just didn't know her blueprint yet. Naming what turns you on — and what doesn't — is one of the most powerful forms of consent literacy you can learn.

Learn Your Erotic Blueprint

The Erotic Blueprints describe five erotic types: Energetic, Sensual, Sexual, Taboo, and Shapeshifter. Each has superpowers and shadows. None is better or worse. Knowing your type doesn't limit you — it frees you.

Lillith's experience shows how mismatched erotic expectations can trip even the most well-intentioned people. The point of understanding your blueprint isn't to sort yourself into a box — it's to understand the conditions under which your body actually says yes. Once you get clear on that, it becomes much easier to spot compatibility. Let's start with the most subtle of the erotic types.

Energetic

Energetics thrive on anticipation, tension, subtlety, breath, longing. They get turned on by what might happen, not what's happening right now. Eye contact, teasing, space between bodies — these are the erotic playgrounds of the Energetic.

Energetics needs time. They need mood. They need alignment. The stars have to decide they're in support of the encounter. Energetics often don't love play parties or chaotic sexual environments; they prefer a slow burn, gentle build, quiet intimacy.

Superpower: They notice everything. Every breath, every shift in energy, every micro-expression. They're world-class teases.

Shadow: They're often overlooked. In group settings, Energetics can be misread as cold, shy, uninterested, or standoffish when really they're just overwhelmed by too much too soon.

Sensual

If Energetics live in the world of anticipation and subtlety, Sensuals live in the world of richness, texture, and pleasure through the senses. For them, eroticism begins long before clothes come off. It begins with atmosphere.

Sensuals are turned on through the senses — touch, taste, smell, sound, aesthetics, atmosphere. They need intentionality and care. Lighting matters. Music matters. Your scent matters. Your sheets matter.

A sensual lover wants to know you've put effort into the environment, not because they're high maintenance, but because sensory input is how their body relaxes enough to become erotic.

▲ Fuck Up: Lack of preparation

Dan was a talented musician with a good heart — and the personal hygiene standards of a man who kept missing the reminder that showers exist. He didn't believe in deodorant, wore clothes that lived on the floor, and his apartment looked like a "before" photo from a home makeover show. Dan couldn't figure out why sensual partners ghosted after the first date.

It wasn't him. It was his aroma.

Superpower: Sensuals are thoughtful lovers. They craft experiences filled with richness, beauty, and presence.

Shadow: Their disappointment is real when someone doesn't meet them in that same intentionality. High standards, unmet expectations, sensory overwhelm — these can get in the way.

Sexual

Sexuals are straightforward: they want sex. Not metaphors. Not build up. Not conversation-as-foreplay. Just pure, unadulterated sex. Sexuals tend to be widely compatible and easy to read.

You'll spot them at parties — they're the first to start playing and the least confused about what they want. They might say things like, "This is great, but can we stop talking and start touching?"

▲ Fuck Up: One track mind

Jack thrived in swinger environments. He was confident, enthusiastic, easy going, and routinely described as a "stunt cock" in group settings (lovingly). While the nickname was meant playfully, it also reflected how narrowly people experienced him.

But when he tried to date in polyamorous circles, he crashed and burned.

People wanted emotional depth, not just sexuality. They wanted vulnerability, curiosity, conversation. Jack didn't yet know how to switch gears. He could offer sex, but not emotional presence.

<u>Superpower</u>: Sexuals are accessible, passionate, and direct, with uncomplicated erotic energy.

<u>Shadow</u>: They may appear insensitive or overly forward to those needing more nuance or emotional pacing.

Taboo

Of course, not everyone is wired for simplicity. Some people don't just want sex; they want the risk, the story, the scene, the delicious thrill of crossing into forbidden territory. Enter the Taboo blueprint.

Taboo types are turned on by the forbidden, the edgy, the unconventional, the power dynamic, the fantasy, or the roleplay. They often enjoy BDSM, kink, fetish play, and anything that stretches the boundaries of sexual norms.

They're creative, imaginative, and often incredible scene partners.

Taboo energy can unlock some of the most exhilarating erotic experiences, but this also requires skill, consent literacy, and emotional maturity. When someone charges into taboo territory without nuance, things can go sideways fast.

▲ Fuck Up: Jekyll and Hyde

Alastair was a brilliant executive — polished, articulate, impressive. But sexually, he became the least favorite person in poly circles. He assumed all female partners wanted to be submissive. He adopted a dominant persona without consent, nuance, or attunement. He bulldozed scenes and ignored cues.

Eventually he was quietly removed from multiple communities.

He wasn't malicious, but he lacked the consent skills and

emotional literacy required to express taboo desires safely.

Superpower: Their creativity and understanding of consent-based frameworks can make encounters deeply fulfilling and artistic.

Shadow: They may become consumed by fantasy, lose connection to reality, or misread partners entirely.

Shapeshifter

While some people anchor deeply into one erotic mode, others find themselves turned on by just about everything. Not because they're fickle, but because they genuinely have the capacity to experience pleasure across multiple erotic languages. These are the Shapeshifters.

Shapeshifters often seem like the easiest blueprint to be in relationship with because they can adapt so well. But that flexibility comes with a hidden challenge. When you can match anyone's energy, it becomes alarmingly easy to disappear into other people's desires without realizing you've lost track of your own.

Shapeshifter's greatest strength can also become their biggest trap.

▲ Fuck Up: The Human Mirror

Maura was a Shapeshifter in the truest sense. She could match anyone's erotic vibe so seamlessly that people often described her as "perfect," "incredible," "my ideal lover," or the deeply confusing "how did you know exactly what I wanted?"

Which was flattering... at first.

Her flexibility meant she blended easily into any dynamic: sensual and slow with one partner, energetic and teasing with another, kinky and experimental with a third. She was brilliant at becoming what people needed. The problem was that no one realized Maura didn't know what she needed.

For months, she drifted through relationships like a mirror. Her lovers felt seen. Maura felt... nothing. Not bad, not good — just disconnected in a way she couldn't name. She thought being able to please everyone was a gift. It was, but it also came with a shadow she didn't want to look at.

The breaking point came during a weekend retreat with three partners, each from a different corner of her relational ecosystem. By midday Saturday she'd shifted through five different erotic modes: sensual-cozy, sexual-direct, energetic-teasing, taboo-curious, and back to sexual again because someone else wanted that.

Halfway through the evening, someone asked an innocent question: "What do you want, Maura?"

She froze. Her brain went blank. Her body went blank. She couldn't answer because she had no idea. She had spent so much time shapeshifting that she had forgotten she had desires separate from the people she loved.

The fuck up wasn't her adaptability. It was abandoning herself inside it.

When she finally admitted she didn't know her own blueprint

needs, the shame hit surprisingly hard. But that moment became a turning point. She realized being a Shapeshifter didn't mean "have no preferences" — it meant having many, and learning which ones actually belonged to her.

Now, she tells every new lover: "I can meet you where you are, but I won't disappear in the process."

It changed everything.

Superpower: Shapeshifters are adaptable. They're erotic Swiss Army knives — multi-talented, curious, and able to fit into most scenarios.

Shadow: It can be hard to tell what they personally want. Because they're so fluid, lovers sometimes struggle to understand their specific turn-ons, not just their responsive ones.

Shapeshifters can be incredible lovers and partners, but their journey is often about learning to stay connected to themselves. On the other end of the spectrum are people whose erotic wiring begins in the mind rather than the body. Enter the sapiosexual.

Sapiosexual

Sapiosexuals are turned on by intellect, depth, curiosity, thoughtfulness, unexpected insights, and emotional nuance. For some, eroticism begins in the mind long before it reaches the body. They want conversation, questions, ideas — something that sparks the neuron before attempting to spark the nipple.

But like every blueprint, sapiosexuality has its shadows too.

▲ Fuck Up: The Debate Club Date

Evan identified as a sapiosexual long before he even knew the word existed. He loved ideas. He loved depth. He loved the spark that came when someone challenged him intellectually. So when he matched with Nora — PhD candidate, philosophy nerd, and someone who used "epistemology" correctly in her bio — he thought he'd found his soulmate.

Their first date started strong. They dove into books, politics, neuroscience, and the ethics of non-monogamy. Evan was enthralled. Nora was brilliant, articulate, and passionate. His body lit up in ways he rarely experienced on a first meeting. But somewhere between the second drink and the third topic shift, Evan's enthusiasm tipped into intensity. Every idea Nora had, he had a counterpoint. Every belief she shared, he challenged. He wasn't trying to dominate her — he thought he was flirting. To him, debate was foreplay. To Nora... it was exhausting.

She was looking for connection, not a dissertation defense. What felt erotic to Evan felt combative to Nora. By the time the check arrived, she was drained, and Evan was confused why she suddenly seemed distant.

A second date never happened.

Evan walked away thinking she "couldn't handle intellectual intimacy." But the truth was simpler. He didn't know how to read the room — or her nervous system. He made conversation a battleground instead of a bridge.

He realized later that sapiosexuality isn't just about loving smart people. It's about knowing how your intelligence interacts with someone else's body, emotions, and boundaries.

Superpower: Sapiosexuals can create erotically charged conversations that feel intimate, connective, and deeply stimulating.

Shadow: They can accidentally become condescending, pedantic, or competitive, mistaking intellectual sparring for intimacy. Without awareness, they'll talk someone into numbness.

Cognitive chemistry is powerful, but it isn't the only relational slow-burn out there. Some people need emotional connection — not intellect, not physicality — for desire to turn on at all.

Demisexual

Demisexuality is one of the most misunderstood erotic styles, especially in communities where spontaneous desire is often assumed to be the norm. Without context, their pace can be misread entirely. And that misunderstanding can turn tender moments into painful ones very quickly.

Demisexuals need emotional connection or situational safety before their desire turns on. They don't perform for others, and they don't experience consistent attraction. Desire is highly contextual.

▲ Fuck Up: The Assumed Yes

Theo was a gentle, thoughtful, intensely emotional man — a classic demisexual. Attraction for him arrived slowly, like light creeping across a room at sunrise. He didn't "just want sex"; he wanted connection, presence, emotional safety. When he had those, he was an incredible lover. When he didn't, his body simply shut down.

The problem? No one told Kai that.

Kai was energetic, impulsive, flirty, and deeply enthusiastic about polyamory. When they started dating, Kai thought Theo's careful pacing was mysterious — even sexy. But after a few weeks, enthusiasm turned into impatience.

During a play party, Kai assumed Theo would eventually "warm up" if he kept encouraging him. He danced on him, kissed his neck, grabbed his hand, whispered about slipping into one of the side rooms "for a minute." Theo tried to smile through it, wanting to be agreeable. His body, however, was staging a full protest.

Later that night, Kai said, "I just don't understand why you didn't want to do anything. I thought you liked me."

That was the moment Theo cracked. Through tears, he said, "I do like you. My nervous system just doesn't work like that."

It wasn't a rejection, disinterest or a lack of desire. It was simply the way his erotic blueprint functioned.

Kai's misstep? Assuming desire is predictable, consistent, and responsive to pressure.

Demisexuals aren't turned on by scenarios. They're turned on by people — specific people, in specific moments, under specific emotional conditions.

Once they finally talked honestly, they rebuilt something gentler and far more real. Kai learned to ask instead of assume. Theo learned that "no" didn't disappoint the right partner — it helped the right partner understand him better. Their dynamic became sweeter, safer, and more grounded than either expected.

And they never repeated the play party incident again.

Superpower: When a demisexual opens to you, the connection can be profound, intentional, and deeply intimate.

Shadow: Their situational desire can be misunderstood, and partners may take inconsistency personally if they don't understand the blueprint.

Every blueprint comes with its gifts and its pitfalls, and none of them are universally compatible on their own. The real magic happens when you learn your blueprint, learn your partner's, and figure out how to meet in the middle with curiosity and care.

♥ Exercise: Take the Quiz

To complete the quiz at no cost,
visit www.polyagony.com/blueprintquiz.

If you want a quick way to start that conversation take the Erotic Blueprint quiz. Invite your partners, lovers, metamours, or future partners to do the same. Then talk about what you learned. What turns you on? What shuts you down? What helps you relax? What helps you feel safe? How can you meet each other where your blueprints overlap — and where they don't?

This conversation alone can transform your erotic connection and deepen intimacy across every relationship you have.

Closing Reflection

Before you apply any of these labels to your sex life, talk about them with the person you're already in relationship with.

Share what blueprint you think you might be.

Ask them what resonates for them.

Notice where your desires overlap and where they don't.

Erotic compatibility isn't about matching perfectly. It's about understanding each other well enough to create safety, excitement, and consent at the same time.

That conversation is the real beginning of a shared erotic life, in polyamory or otherwise.

Chapter 4
Communication Styles

"The single biggest problem in communication
is the illusion that it has taken place."

George Bernard Shaw, *Man and Superman*

The most common word in this book series is, without a doubt, communication. Not because it sounds enlightened, but because it's where most polyamorous fuck-ups usually happen. People think they're communicating when what they're really doing is assuming, reacting, narrating, spiraling, or talking at someone instead of with them.

Healthy communication isn't about scripts or the perfect tone. It begins with two simple things: curiosity and willingness. The philosophy I come back to again and again — in my own relationships, in my communities, and in every article I write — is this:

Be Curious and Communicate.

Curiosity softens defensiveness. Communication creates connection. Together, they turn conflict from a battlefield into a conversation.

Curiosity sounds like:

"Help me understand what you're feeling."

"I want to know what's underneath that."

"Can you tell me what this brought up for you?"

Communication sounds like:

"Here's what's happening for me."

"I'm feeling overwhelmed and need reassurance."

"I'm not upset with you — I'm scared."

Polyamory requires presence. And presence comes from two commitments: staying curious and staying connected. Most people skip curiosity entirely and go straight to conclusions. Many people communicate only once they're already hurt.

Polyamory is far easier to navigate when curiosity comes first — and communication flows before the meltdown, not after it.

People love to say "communication is key," but very few talk about how to actually do it when you're scared, jealous, overwhelmed, triggered, or crying in a Whole Foods parking lot. Polyamory doesn't just test your communication; it magnifies every crack in it.

So before we get into scripts or tools, start with something simple: know your own style.

♥ Exercise: Know how you communicate

To see a more fulsome communication challenge,
visit www.polyagony.com/communicationchallenge.

Before engaging with others, ask yourself:

- ▶ How do I communicate when I'm grounded?
- ▶ How do I communicate when I'm stressed?
- ▶ What happens when my nervous system is triggered?
- ▶ Do I avoid?
- ▶ Do I shut down?
- ▶ Do I get clingy or anxious?
- ▶ Do I go silent and stew?
- ▶ Do I lash out?
- ▶ Do I talk too much? Not enough?
- ▶ Do I demand clarity? Or withdraw from conflict?

You don't need to fix anything yet. Just know your pattern. Awareness is the difference between saying, "This is who I am right now, please handle with care," and accidentally damaging a perfectly good relationship because you thought your panic was communication.

Multiamory's Four Pillars of Healthy Non-Monogamy

The *Multiamory Podcast* (multiamory.com with Emily Matlack, Dedeker Winston, and Jase Lindgren) describes four foundational principles that support healthy non-monogamy: communication, honesty, trust, and respect. They're simple, but not easy.

Communication

Open, ongoing dialogue about feelings, boundaries, expectations, and emotional needs. Not once, not annually, but regularly and compassionately.

▶ Ask yourself: Am I prepared to communicate consistently with the people I love?

Honesty

Truth about your desires, fears, needs, limits, and motivations. Honesty isn't about dumping raw feelings onto people; it's about sharing what's relevant for connection and clarity.

▶ Ask yourself: Can I express truths that might disappoint someone? Can I hear truths that might sting?

Trust

Built through consistent actions, reliability, and integrity. Polyamory magnifies whatever trust issues are already present — it doesn't fix them.

▶ Ask yourself: Do I keep my word? Do the people around me?

Respect

A recognition that your partners are full human beings with

their own needs, emotions, limits, and autonomy. Respect is what makes a "no" still feel safe.

▶ Ask yourself: Can I honor someone's boundaries, even when they diverge from my own desires?

Use these pillars as a quiet check-in with yourself before adding new complexity to your relational ecosystem. They're not rules; they're stabilizers.

♥ **Exercise: Am I ready?**

To see a more detailed quiz to determine if you are ready to begin dating, visit www.polyagony.com/amiready.

Before dating others, ask yourself:

▶ **Communication:** Am I willing to have uncomfortable but necessary conversations?

▶ **Honesty:** Can I tell the truth without managing the other person's emotions?

▶ **Trust:** Have I built relational consistency? Do I extend trust too quickly? Too slowly?

▶ **Respect:** Am I willing to honor someone's autonomy even when it conflicts with my desires?

Your answers don't have to be perfect. They just need to be real.

Active Listening and Nonviolent Communication

One of the most effective communication tools in polyamory is active listening — the art of truly hearing someone instead of waiting for your turn to talk. It requires presence, curiosity, and the humility to recognize that your partner's internal world is not the same as yours.

The Multiamory Podcast explores this beautifully in their episode on active listening: where communication becomes less about being right and more about understanding what's happening underneath the words.

Another powerful tool is Nonviolent Communication (NVC), developed by Marshall Rosenberg in ***Nonviolent Communication: A Language of Life*** (2003). NVC helps you express your needs without blame, accusation, or emotional landmines. Instead of "You never consider me," it becomes, "When this happened, I felt disconnected and needed reassurance." It sounds simple, but it changes everything. And speaking of reassurance...

▲ Fuck Up: It's never about the chores

Savannah didn't think she was bad at communication; she thought she was organized. Whenever her partner Tom returned from a date with someone else, she'd wake up the next morning and launch into a domestic whirlwind.

"Can you take out the trash?" "And mop the floor?" "And why didn't you fold the towels?" "And why is your backpack still by the couch?"

Tom thought she was nitpicking. Savannah thought she was communicating.

Neither was correct.

Savannah wasn't angry about the laundry. She was anxious about connection.

The chores were a smokescreen for fear: fear of being replaced, fear of not mattering, fear that Tom's intimacy with someone else meant less intimacy with her. But instead of saying, "I feel scared and I need closeness after your dates," she gave him a to-do list long enough to qualify as manual labor.

Tom missed the pattern entirely. And Savannah spiraled every time.

Had they slowed down long enough to name the fear beneath the micro-management, they could have saved a year of pointless fights — and several Saturdays of work.

This is the heart of communication breakdown: the thing we're yelling about is rarely the thing we're actually hurt about.

Savannah and Tom's dynamic is a classic example of how communication breaks down when curiosity is missing. If either of them had paused long enough to ask, "What's really going on underneath this reaction?" the entire cycle could have shifted. This is why I always return to the same relational rule: be curious first, communicate second. (www.consentculture.community)

Curiosity opens the door. Communication walks you through it.

NVC + Active Listening in Practice

Using NVC and active listening could have changed Savannah and Tom's entire dynamic.

Instead of chore lists, Savannah could have said:

> "I feel anxious when you come home from a date and go straight into your own world. I need connection or reassurance to help my nervous system settle."

Instead of defensiveness, Tom could have said:

> "What I hear you saying is that you need closeness, not perfection."

Suddenly, they're partners again — not opponents.

♥ Exercise: Communication Check-In

> To see a sample agenda and talking point prompts
> for a check-in, visit www.polyagony.com/checkin.

To build stronger communication before you open up, consider the following process:

1. **Set a Time:** Pick a weekly or biweekly check-in that's sacred and uninterrupted.

2. **Use a Talking Stick (or object):** Whoever holds the object speaks. Everyone else listens.

3. **Use NVC**

    Observation: "When I noticed..."

    Feeling: "...I felt..."

    Need: "...because I need..."

    Request: "Would you be willing to...?"

4. **Active Listening:** Reflect back what you heard: "What I think you're saying is..."

5. **Discuss & Adjust:** Collaborate on how to meet each other's needs moving forward.

Practicing this when things are calm makes it infinitely easier when things are tender.

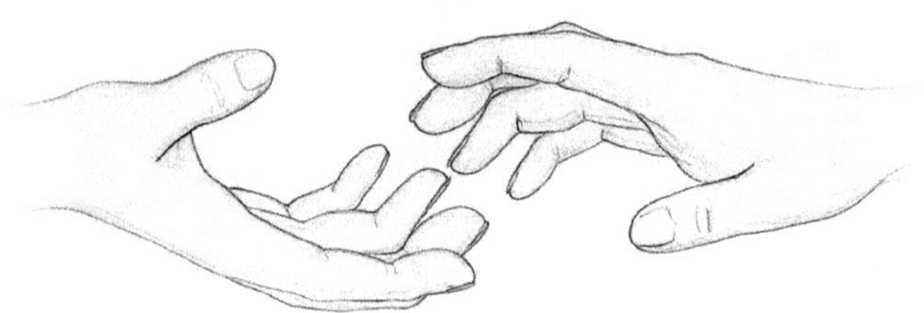

Chapter 5
Attachment Style

"All of us, from cradle to grave, are happiest when life is organized as a series of excursions, long or short, from the secure base provided by our attachment figures."

John Bowlby, *A Secure Base*

If there's one concept that shows up over and over again in open relating — quietly shaping your reactions, your insecurities, and your relational instincts — it's attachment. Not just the theory, but the lived reality of how your nervous system responds to closeness, distance, uncertainty, intimacy, and change.

After more than fifteen years of navigating open relationships, I've learned this: secure attachment is the backbone of sustainable non-monogamy. When you trust your partner and they trust you, everything else becomes infinitely easier. Jealousy softens. Communication deepens. You feel more grounded in yourself and more connected to each other.

Secure attachment doesn't mean never feeling insecure. It means that when insecurity hits, you don't assume the world is ending.

If you want to explore this topic further, I strongly recommend *Polysecure* by Jessica Fern (Fern, 2020). It's the groundwork for a deeper, trauma-informed, non-monogamy-aware understanding of attachment. This chapter won't attempt to recreate Fern's entire book, but we'll touch on the pieces that matter most as you step into (or deepen) your open relationships.

What Secure Attachment Looks Like in Practice

Girard and Corrina have been together for nine years and married for eight. They have raised a daughter together, survived stressful seasons, celebrated beautiful ones, and built a partnership that didn't start secure but became secure through a lot of learning, repairing, unlearning, and trying again.

She's a licensed therapist — not the glossy Instagram kind, but the real, grounded, steady kind. The kind who can hold hard emotions without flinching. She's been Girard's bedrock through his entire journey into ethical non-monogamy. Long before he had language for attachment theory, she was quietly showing him how to build it: how to communicate honestly, how to stay in connection when things felt uncomfortable, how to repair conflict instead of disappearing from it.

He wasn't always good at that. But she modeled it over and over until it became part of him, part of the way he moved in relationships.

Today, their relationship feels deeply secure. When Girard

goes away for a week with his partner, Corrina isn't threatened by it. She doesn't brace for loss or abandonment. She trusts him — and he trusts her — because they have spent years building that trust, brick by brick.

And that support isn't magic. It isn't effortless. And it definitely didn't fall out of the sky fully formed.

It came from conversations neither of them wanted to have at first, arguments they didn't handle well the first time, moments of tenderness in the middle of the mess, and a shared decision not to give up on curiosity when defensiveness would have been easier.

Secure attachment doesn't remove jealousy, fear, or discomfort. It gives you the tools and the resilience to navigate them.

But here's the catch: the secure attachment you build with one partner doesn't automatically transfer to every new lover.

Every new connection begins without a shared history. You don't know yet how they handle conflict. You don't know whether they communicate consistently or disappear when overwhelmed. You don't know if they'll respond well to vulnerability, or shut down, or ramp up. Your nervous system doesn't have a track record to lean on.

Which is why knowing your own attachment style before you start dating new partners is one of the kindest things you can do — for yourself and for them.

▲ Fuck Up: I forgot that I'm anxious

In the safety of his marriage with Corrina, Girard thought of himself as secure. He didn't worry that she would leave if she went on a date. He didn't spiral when she texted back late. He felt solid and grounded in their bond. For years, there was no reason to question that.

Then he started seeing his first new lover. Suddenly, a very different version of himself emerged.

He became hypervigilant. He checked his phone constantly. A delayed reply made his stomach twist. If she didn't text back quickly, his mind sprinted ahead to worst-case scenarios. He lost sleep waiting for a message. He reread conversations obsessively, hunting for reassurance between the lines. When she went quiet for a few hours, he felt physically sick — even while telling himself she was probably busy.

He didn't recognize himself. He was overwhelmed.

Eventually, he ended the relationship. Not because she was wrong for him, but because his own anxiety swallowed him whole.

Only later did he see what had happened. His attachment style hadn't magically changed. The context had.

He felt secure with Corrina because that relationship had years of proof behind it. But in new dynamics, his underlying anxious attachment traits came roaring back. The old fear of being abandoned, not chosen, or "too much" had simply been sleeping, not gone.

If Girard had understood and communicated his attachment style from the start, he and his new lover could have co-created something more supportive: explicit reassurance, predictable check-ins, clarity around expectations. Instead, he was blindsided by his own nervous system.

Knowing your attachment style doesn't make the hard feelings vanish. It helps you understand them, plan for them, and communicate about them before they run the show.

Attachment isn't only about how you show up at the beginning of a connection; it also shapes how relationships evolve over time. As partners grow, individuate, and build parallel lives (as discussed in Book 3) — something that becomes especially important in long-term non-monogamy dynamics — your attachment style influences how you handle shifting needs, different levels of intimacy, changing schedules, and the natural ebb and flow of connection.

People who understand their attachment patterns tend to navigate these transitions with more resilience and less fear. Those who don't can end up clinging, retreating, or spiraling when relationships deepen, plateau, or transform. The work you do here, in understanding your attachment needs, becomes the foundation for everything explored later in the individuation and relationship evolution chapters.

♥ **Exercise: Learn your attachment style**

To learn exercises for building secure attachment as an adult, visit www.polyagony.com/secureattachment.

Rate each of the following statements from 1 to 5 and write down your score:

1 = Strongly disagree, 5 = Strongly agree

1. I often worry that my partner doesn't love me as much as I love them.

2. I feel comfortable depending on others and having them depend on me.

3. I find it difficult to trust others completely.

4. I prefer not to rely on others and keep my distance emotionally.

5. I often feel anxious when I'm not in contact with my partner.

6. I am comfortable with intimacy and find it easy to get close to others.

7. I become very upset when my partner is not available or is busy.

8. I avoid getting too close to others to protect myself from being hurt.

9. I feel secure in my relationships and rarely worry about my partner's feelings for me.

10. I often feel that my partner is too clingy or needy.

Scoring

Tally your scores in the following combinations, and notice where you have the highest score:

Anxious indicators: Items 1, 5, 7
Secure indicators: Items 2, 6, 9
Avoidant indicators: Items 3, 4, 8, 10

Once you've found your pattern, reflect on these:

▶ How does this style show up in your relationships?

▶ What situations activate it the most?

▶ What would help your nervous system feel safer in new dynamics?

▶ What do you need to tell new partners so they can support you?

▶ What do future partners deserve to know about how you attach?

▶ And most importantly: How can you practice secure behaviors even if your attachment isn't secure yet?

Attachment style is not a sentence handed down from on high. It's a map.

And maps are especially useful when the relational terrain gets complicated — as it often does in open relating. As your relationships evolve, individuate, and change shape over time (something we'll explore in more depth in Book 3), understanding your attachment needs will help you navigate those transitions with far more grace and far less chaos.

Part Two:

Preparing Your Partnership

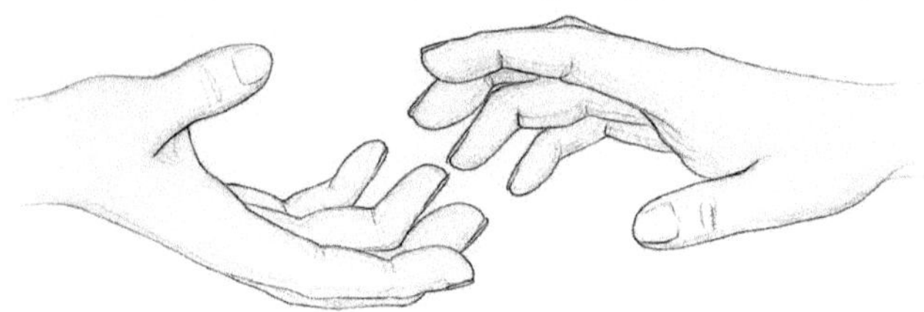

Chapter 6
Un-monogomize Yourself -
Engaging with Partners/Lovers

"Trouble looms when monogamy is no longer a free expression of loyalty but a form of enforced compliance."

Esther Perel, *Mating in Captivity*

You have read the books, listened to the podcasts, had the late night talks, and now you are finally here.

You booked a date with someone who is openly poly. You RSVP'd to your first event. You are excited, nauseous, turned on, and a little bit convinced you might be losing your mind. These feelings are not a red flag. This is what it feels like when theory turns into practice. This is what I lovingly phrase as "the dog who caught the car."

Your body is catching up to your ideas. Your nervous system is trying to understand what your mouth has just agreed to. The work now is not to make the feelings go away. The work is to give those feelings somewhere to land, so you can move through this new terrain with care instead of chaos. If you are already coupled, this work starts at home.

Forming Agreements

"We find comfort among those who agree with us - growth among those who don't."

Frank A. Clark

Agreements are not just a polyamory thing. They sit under every relationship you have ever had. They form the backbone of healthy, respectful, and fulfilling relationships in any context. In open relating, they're even more important. Without them, you end up stepping on invisible landmines and wondering why everything suddenly hurts.

Research on consensual non-monogamy shows that clear communication and mutual understanding are essential for relationship satisfaction. (A.C. Moors, J.D. Rubin, J.L. Matsick, A. Ziegler, & T.D. Conley Journal of Sex Research 2014/2015) In a culture that loves to romanticize "love without limits," it's easy to forget that real people, with real nervous systems, need clarity to feel safe and avoid misunderstandings.

Agreements aren't meant to be a cage. They're meant to be a container. They hold things like: How you protect sexual health. How you protect emotional safety. How you manage time and energy. Who knows what about your life.

Not as rules thrown down by the most scared person in the room, but as shared choices you both consent to.
When you do not name agreements, people fill the silence with their fears.

▲ Fuck Up: Thrown into the deep end

Ariel and Gustavo had been dating for a few months when they decided to go to a sex club together. Gustavo had been in the swinger scene for years and felt right at home. Ariel was new to all of it.

They didn't talk much beforehand. No conversations about what Ariel might see. No discussion of what they might do together. No time spent on fears or boundaries. Gustavo figured she'd be fine once she got there. Ariel, meanwhile, was quietly tying herself into emotional knots.

In the days leading up to their night out, Ariel's anxiety grew. She worried that Gustavo might leave her for someone he met there. She worried about STIs. She worried about being pressured into acts she didn't want. She worried about freezing and not knowing how to say no.

She made herself physically sick with worry on the day of the event — but didn't say anything, afraid of ruining his excitement.

Gustavo didn't ask. He was avoidant and thought, "I'll just bring her and let her feel it out."

At the club, Ariel was clingy. She didn't know how to navigate the space or the people. Gustavo quickly slipped into his comfort zone, greeting familiar faces. They both started drinking to cope — Ariel far more than usual. Within an hour, she was drunk.

They ended up in a bedroom with a couple Ariel had just met. There were no real conversations beyond names. As the sexual energy built, Ariel's nervous system crashed. She had a panic attack, started hyperventilating, and eventually vomited all over the scene.

The night collapsed. So did her sense of safety. This wasn't a "she wasn't ready for poly" story. This was a no one prepared her story.

Ariel didn't know how to advocate for herself. Gustavo didn't know how to support her. Neither of them had agreements — with themselves or each other — about what safety looked like.

Studies on Consensual Non-Monogamy (CNM) show that people report higher anxiety and distress when there's a lack of transparency, communication, and shared expectations around new situations. (M. Barker & C. Langdridge 2010/2018) That's not because open relating is inherently chaotic — it's because our nervous systems don't like surprises when our hearts are on the line.

Why Agreements Matter More Than Vibes

> "Healthy boundaries are not walls.
> They are the gates and fences that allow you
> to enjoy the beauty of your own garden."
>
> attributed to **Lydia H. Hall** (SSJE, 2018)

At the heart of polyamory is the belief that love is not a finite resource. (See C. Klesse 2016 for more on the ideology of love abundance in polyamory.) You can care for more than one person without diminishing your connection to anyone else.

But that abundance doesn't cancel out the need for boundaries. Well-defined agreements support:

emotional safety
"What do we do if one of us gets triggered?"

sexual safety
"What are our safer sex practices?"

time safety
"How do we divide time without burning out?"

Research suggests that when partners consciously negotiate agreements in CNM, they experience more emotional and sexual satisfaction. (A.C. Moors, J.D. Rubin, J.L. Matsick, A. Ziegler, & T.D. Conley *Journal of Sex Research* 2014/2015)

Because agreements are not just about limits — they're about making everyone feel considered.

♥ **Exercise: Mapping Your Agreements Landscape**

See a detailed interactive agreement landscape at
www.polyagony.com/agreementmapping.

Find a quiet moment and sit with these questions — write, speak them aloud, or voice-note your way through them. The point is to hear your own truth without rushing.

Start with yourself.

▶ Ask: What agreements do I have with myself right

now? Where are my own boundaries, promises, and non-negotiables? What keeps me grounded and emotionally safe?

Next, move to the relationships already in your life.

▶ Ask: What agreements do we currently have as a couple (if in an existing partnership), and which ones need to be clarified or created? What helps us stay connected? What feels unclear or assumed that needs to be spoken aloud?

Then imagine relationships to come.

▶ Ask: What agreements would I need with future partners to feel safe, steady, and able to open my heart? What structures help you relax instead of brace? What clarity helps you show up authentically?

Take your time. You're not drafting a 20-page constitution. You're sketching the scaffolding that lets you — and everyone who loves you — breathe easier, explore more freely, and enjoy the connections you're building.

Remember: Agreements are the scaffolding, not the prison.

Creating Guidance for Self

"You have to love yourself before you can love anyone else."

Ivar (author's son, age 6)

Before you can engage meaningfully with anyone else in polyamory, you have to know yourself — really know yourself.

Self-awareness is not a poly bonus feature. It is the oxygen mask.

Research on CNM and relationship satisfaction keeps pointing back to the same idea: people who know their own needs and boundaries weather the storms of non-monogamy with far more resilience. (A.C. Moors, J.D. Rubin, J.L. Matsick, A. Ziegler, & T.D. Conley *Journal of Sex Research* 2014/2015)

Your boundaries. Your needs. Your limits. Your desires. Your capacity. Your quirks. Your triggers. Your pace.

When you understand yourself, agreements become clarity, not control. Connection becomes easier. And you're less likely to find yourself crying in a bathroom, overwhelmed by a situation you didn't know how to navigate.

Had Ariel taken even ten minutes to reflect on her fears and boundaries before entering that sex club, she could have communicated them to Gustavo — and protected herself from panic, shame, and literal nausea.

Had Gustavo taken the time to ask her what she needed, he might have realized she didn't feel safe being thrown into the deep end and could have paced their night very differently. Knowing yourself doesn't just support you. It protects everyone involved.

The RBDSMA Formula: Start With Yourself First

RBDSMA is an effective and familiar tool in polyamorous environments — a quick way for people to communicate their boundaries and desires. However, I find it helpful to first have this discussion with yourself to understand your boundaries and desires, before you attempt to share them with anyone else.

Think of it as your internal agreements list — a blueprint for how you want to show up in the world.

♥ Exercise: Complete your personal RBDSMA

Take a moment to write your answers to each of the following:

R: Relationship Status and Agreements

How would you describe your current relational landscape? Are you partnered, solo poly, dating casually, relationship saturated, open but not looking, something else entirely? What agreements already exist in your world?
Clarity here is not about picking the "right" label. It is about helping your future lovers understand where they fit and what is already true in your life. Studies on CNM show that clear orientation around structure reduces misunderstandings and boosts satisfaction. (A.C. Moors, J.D. Rubin, J.L. Matsick, A. Ziegler, & T.D. Conley *Journal of Sex Research* 2014/2015)

B: Boundaries

What are you a no to right now?

That might be specific acts, certain substances, particular environments, time of night, emotional labor, frequency of dates, or anything else that leaves you drained or dysregulated.

Boundaries aren't about controlling others. They're about caring for yourself – clear boundaries dramatically increase emotional safety. (See M. Barker & C. Langdridge 2010/2018: "Non-monogamies" and other CNM-focused work illustrating distress when communication/clarity is lacking)

D: Desires

What are you a yes to?

What kind of intimacy lights you up? What experiences are you curious about? Are you craving depth, play, casual exploration, kink, romance, affection, conversation, group scenes, one on one?

This is your chance to articulate what nourishes you. Research suggests that naming desires — even privately — increases fulfillment and reduces shame. (Klesse 2016: Research on desire, identity, and sexual meaning in poly communities)

S: Sexual Health and Safety

When were you last tested, and for what? What were the results?

What safer sex practices do you want as non-negotiables with new partners? How do you feel about fluid bonding? How do you relate to consent if substances are involved?

Open communication about sexual health is one of the

strongest predictors of trust and satisfaction in CNM relationships. (See Bibby et al., 2025)

M: Meaning

What does sex, connection, and dating mean to you?
Are one night stands fun or hollow? Do you tend to attach quickly? Do you bond quickly? Do you dissociate if things feel casual? Do you want lovers, partners, friends-with-benefits, or relationship escalators?

Understanding the meaning you attach to encounters helps prevent mismatches — and heartbreak. (M. Barker & C. Langdridge 2010/2018)

A: Aftercare

What helps your body come back to earth, helps you feel regulated and connected after intensity?
Do you need cuddles, a snack, a follow up text, space, a debrief, plans for next time, a shower alone, a meme?
Aftercare is not just for kink. It stabilizes your nervous system and deepens trust, especially when experiences are intense or vulnerable. (M. Barker & C. Langdridge 2010/2018)

Why This Matters

The RBDSMA formula serves not only as a guideline for interacting with others but also as a reflective tool for establishing your own agreements with yourself.

When you know your own boundaries, desires, meaning,

and aftercare needs, you become more grounded, more confident, more prepared, more honest, more discerning, more generous, more emotionally available.

You reduce the likelihood of reactive behavior. You reduce avoidant communication. You reduce the "I didn't know how to ask for what I needed" spiral.

Know yourself clearly. Love yourself deliberately. Then bring that clarity into your relationships.

Remember: your journey into polyamory starts with the commitments you make to yourself, paving the way for meaningful interactions with others. Everything else flows from here.

Aligning with Existing Partners

> "Coming together is a beginning;
> keeping together is progress;
> working together is success."

Henry Ford

Once you've taken yourself through the RBDSMA, the next step is to bring that clarity into conversation with your partner.

Before diving into the structured part, though, it's incredibly helpful to start with something softer — something that gets both nervous systems in the room.

♥ Exercise: Wildest and Mildest

I recommend a game that I call "wildest and mildest," something I learned from a friend and sex educator, Reid Mihalko.

To see Reid explain how to conduct this game,
visit www.polyagony.com/wildestandmildest.

Sit down together and ask:

► What are my wildest hopes as we open up?

► What are my mildest hopes?

► What are my wildest fears?

► And what are my mildest fears?

Let yourselves be honest. Maybe your wildest hope is finding another long-term partner.

Maybe your wildest hope is finding another long-term partner. Maybe it's exploring bisexuality, or finally feeling sexually expressed in ways monogamy never allowed.

Say the quiet things out loud. Hopes create openings — they show you what you're moving toward, not just what you're avoiding.

Research shows that sharing positive aspirations strengthens emotional bonds and increases satisfaction in relationships. (Gable & Reis, 2010; Otto et al., 2014)

Of course, where there are hopes, there are fears.

Maybe you fear losing the comfort of your home base. Maybe you fear the stress of it all — or complicating your existing bond in ways you can't express. Maybe you fear losing the very relationship you are hoping to evolve.

Research on CNM shows that openly discussing fears and insecurities can reduce anxiety and enhance trust between partners (Barker & Langdridge, 2010).

This "wildest and mildest" conversation is the emotional primer that makes the rest of the work easier. Once the hopes and fears are on the table, you can transition into an RBDSMA discussion with far more compassion and clarity.

If Ariel and Gustavo had done this before their night out, Ariel could have voiced her fears — STIs, abandonment, jealousy, mixing sex with alcohol — and Gustavo could have met her where she was instead of dragging her into the deep end with no life jacket. Their night may not have turned into panic, hyperventilating, and vomit on a stranger's duvet, and the two of them would have had an opportunity to discuss how they might help each other to feel safe, which aligns with findings that suggest proactive communication about boundaries and concerns can mitigate potential conflicts and foster mutual understanding. (Ritchie & Barker 2006: on sexual health communication in CNM)

Talking through hopes and fears doesn't make everything easy, but it makes things possible.

It creates a foundation where agreements aren't rigid constraints but shared safety rails — something that lets everyone breathe. These safety rails foster clearer communication which helps you both feel more secure as you navigate your evolving relationship dynamics together, creating a solid foundation of understanding and empathy.

Formalizing Agreements

"Daring to set boundaries is about having the courage to love ourselves, even when we risk disappointing others."

Brené Brown, on *Oprah* 2021

Once you've explored hopes, fears, and personal boundaries, it's time to formalize your actual agreements.

And before anything else, it's important to clarify the following:

Agreements are NOT rules. Rules are imposed. Agreements are chosen.

An agreement is defined as mutual assent to shared terms (Merriam-Webster, n.d.).

Your agreements should never function like handcuffs.

They should function like handrails.

Something you lean on, not something you feel trapped inside.

▲ Fuck Up: Micro-managing via agreements

Diana and Patrick did this dance for years and are a classic study in what not to do. Micro-managing by using uneven agreements.

For years, Patrick had blanket permission to pursue whoever he wanted. Diana, meanwhile, had to get approval for specific acts with specific people. Patrick also held veto power — and he used it. Often.

Diana's world became smaller. Patrick's became bigger.

When Diana asked if she could explore a crush on a work trip, Patrick said he wasn't comfortable with her having oral sex. She backed down. He, in turn, continued dating freely. Over time, resentment built. Diana began acting out, feeling more like a teenager asking for permission than an equal partner.

This is one of the most common early poly fuck-ups: using agreements as a way to manage power – the imbalance reflects common pitfalls in non-monogamous relationships, where one partner may exert control over the other, leading to resentment and dissatisfaction. (Ritchie & Barker 2006)

If you sense a rule is being imposed on you, pause the conversation. If you feel tempted to impose one, pause the conversation.

For nearly a decade, Diana and Patrick lived inside an unhealthy, unbalanced power dynamic disguised as "agreements" that was difficult for them to navigate. They weren't agreements. They were containment strategies.

Create agreements that promote mutual respect and understanding, rather than impose control over one another. This foundation will help ensure that your agreements are supportive and empowering for both partners.

Agreement Evolution Over Time

"The only constant in life is change."

Heraclitus

When interviewing CNM couples for this book, one pattern showed up everywhere, no matter if they were new to open relating or seasoned veterans: early agreements are either nonexistent (planting land mines which create chaos), overly rigid (controlling, or as you've seen rules based), or both.

Rigid agreements serve a purpose at the beginning. They soothe the nervous system while your relationship transitions out of monogamy and into something structurally different. As you grow more secure, the agreements evolve with you. Research consistently shows that CNM partners who revisit and update agreements regularly have higher relational stability and satisfaction. (See Gottman 1994 CNM communication studies and Moors et al., 2015)

I review agreements with my partners quarterly. Some couples do monthly check-ins with a poly-informed therapist. Some do annual recalibrations. Many check in when major life changes happen – i.e. changing jobs, moving house or pregnancy. What matters is consistency.

Early agreements often look like:

"We only play together." "No kissing." "No overnights." "You have to text at midnight." "No sex in our bed."

As time passes, you will likely:

feel safer with one another;

develop secure attachment to partners/metamours;

gain experience and confidence in open relating.

And your agreements will shift.

The point is not perfection. The point is alignment.

Transparency v. Disclosure

"Transparency doesn't mean sharing every detail. Transparency means providing the context for the decisions we make."

Simon Sinek (LinkedIn post, 2018)

One of the most important realizations in open relating is this:

Not everyone needs (or wants) the same amount of information.

Among the 100 people I interviewed for this book, the same words came up over and over: transparency, honesty, integrity. People wanted to feel "in the loop" with partners who date others.

People crave transparency, but not always disclosure.

Those two words get used interchangeably, but they're not the same thing.

Transparency is the big picture:

- ▶ Am I dating someone?
- ▶ Is this purely sexual, emotional, or developing into more?
- ▶ Do I have feelings?
- ▶ Is this relationship important to me?
- ▶ Are there changes in my availability or capacity?

Transparency gives partners the context they need to feel secure. Transparency involves providing a broad understanding of one's feelings, intentions, and relationship dynamics.

Disclosure, on the other hand, is the granular detail, the specifics and facts about interactions with others:

- ▶ Who touched what?
- ▶ What did they say afterward?
- ▶ Did they stay the night?
- ▶ What positions?
- ▶ How many orgasms?
- ▶ What did they eat for breakfast?

Disclosure is often about facts. Transparency is about orientation. Both are valid. Both can be good. Neither is morally superior. The key is knowing which one you need — and which one your partners need.

The Spectrum Between Us

In many relationships, couples will discover that they live on different ends of this spectrum.

One likes details. You want to know when he's going on a date, what unfolded, how he felt, where his heart landed afterward. For you, disclosure reduces anxiety and increases your sense of connection and joy.

Another, on the other hand, prefers a gentle version of Don't Ask Don't Tell (DADT). You want transparency — "Are you out with someone? Are you safe? Are you good?" — but not the play-by-play. Hearing details dysregulates you, and you don't want to carry emotional weight that isn't meaningful to you.

This difference isn't a mismatch. It's a negotiation, and results in an agreement.

They know you're on a date, or at a community event, or traveling with a lover. They know the shape of your emotional world. But they don't want the scenes, scripts, or specifics unless they represent a major relational shift, new feelings, or a safety concern.

It is possible to find a rhythm that honors both of you. That is the purpose of agreements in open relating — not uniformity, but harmony.

This negotiation allows both of you to maintain your individual comfort zones while still fostering a sense of trust and security in your relationship.

Research on non-monogamous relationships shows that unmet expectations around communication style can create tension, anxiety, and avoidable misunderstandings that result in feelings of neglect. (Conley et al. 2013: research on communication expectations in CNM, and see Moors, Ritchie & Barker, and Miller 2013 for disclosure/transparency frameworks)

Not because disclosure is inherently better or worse — but because assumptions create hurt where clarity would have created connection.

One partner might need reassurance, emotional context, and knowledge of milestones.

The other might need privacy, space, autonomy, and clear boundaries around oversharing.

What creates suffering is silence or guessing.

♥ Exercise: Rate your disclosure preference

Find a more detailed explanation of disclosure preferences and trade-offs at www.polyagony.com/disclosure.

Instead of relying on vibes or guessing "how much is too much," use this spectrum to articulate what you want to receive from a partner — and what you want to offer.

Here are the four major positions on the disclosure continuum, on this page and the next:

Disclosure level	Example	Benefits	Drawbacks
DADT	"I'm going out" with no details	Minimizes emotional triggers for the partner who prefers less detail. Reduces pressure for the person dating to "perform honesty" in ways that feel exhausting.	The dating partner may feel like they're hiding or fragmenting parts of their life. The receiving partner may learn details from third parties, creating dysregulation. Can create emotional distance if used reflexively instead of intentionally.
Only share when asked	"Where are you going?" "I'm going to a festival" "Who are you going with? "Stephanie and Arik"	Gives the partner who needs selective information control over timing. Allows honesty without oversharing.	Can feel stifling for the partner who wants to share naturally. If scene dynamics shift mid-date, the person dating may not know whether new information violates the "only when asked" container.

Disclosure level	Example	Benefits	Drawbacks
Share at specific threshold	"We had sex for the first time." "They told me they loved me." Partners agree on what constitutes an update-worthy event.	Protects emotional safety by naming what matters most. Prevents surprises or third-party "snowball moments."	Can create patterns of anxiety around sharing ("Will this trigger them?"), and build fear or shame around the act of sharing May unintentionally reinforce hierarchy if one partner's thresholds differ from another's.
Full Disclosure. Sharing all details.	Self explanatory. This is the "tell me everything" camp	Great for those who experience compersion through detail. Can increase intimacy if both partners enjoy storytelling	Can feel like surveillance if not mutually desired. May violate the privacy of other partners who didn't consent to their intimacy being shared.

Now, write down — separately, then together — your preferences for:

▶ How much do I want to know?

▶ How much do I want to share?

▶ What details make me feel secure?

▶ What details overwhelm me?

▶ What counts as "significant enough" to disclose?

▶ Do I prefer transparency + broad strokes, or transparency + detail?

It is entirely valid to say, "I don't want to know the details" without placing blame on either partner for their preferences.

And most importantly: Do my needs differ depending on the partner involved? Many people discover they want full disclosure from their anchor partner, but only transparency from metamours or secondary partners.

A Note on DADT

Some people judge DADT harshly — as though it's inherently "un-poly" or dishonest. After a decade of living, renegotiating, and growing inside various agreement structures, I can confidently say this:

DADT is not avoidance when it is chosen. It is only avoidance when it replaces emotional work.

If a partner explicitly says, "I don't want details because my nervous system does better without them," that is a need, not a flaw.

If you trust each other, communicate clearly, and negotiate honestly, DADT can be a supportive structure — not a loophole.

Documenting and Revisiting Your Agreements

"The pen is mightier than the sword."

Edward Bulwer-Lytton

Once you've talked through your initial agreements, the next step is deceptively simple and wildly important:

Write them down. Not in your memory. Not in a vague "I'm sure we said something about that" way.

Write. Them. Down.

Put them somewhere you can both access.

A written record provides clarity, accountability, and a way to return to the same page when emotions run high.

Writing agreements down doesn't prevent conflict. It prevents unnecessary conflict.

▲ Fuck Up: Taking off the wedding ring

Dante and Lori had been open for a while and felt "comfortable enough," so they never formalized their agreements. Everything was just… understood. Until it wasn't.

One night, Lori noticed that Dante had taken off his wedding ring during a sensual massage with a new partner. Seeing his bare hand broke something inside of her. She felt disrespected and betrayed, certain he had violated an agreement.

Dante was positive that they had never discussed wedding rings, and removed his simply to avoid it slipping off during the massage.

Here's the thing — they were both telling the truth as they remembered it. But because nothing was written down, they had no shared reference point. The "truth" became two wounded nervous systems arguing about who was right.

Without documentation, fear can masquerade as memory or perceived agreement.

Writing agreements down doesn't prevent conflict - it prevents unnecessary conflict.

♥ **Exercise: Craft your written agreements**

Complete an interactive and ongoing set of written agreements at www.polyagony.com/writtenagreements.

Create a new entry dated today. Write out three things:

1. **What we need from each other**
   Examples: share intentions before a date, kiss goodbye before leaving, text if a date will run past midnight, use condoms for penetrative sex, shower before getting into our shared bed, cuddle or reconnect when we're back together.

2. **Hard boundaries**
   Examples: no overnights without discussion, no sex in our shared bed, no showers with new partners, no sex if RBDSMA reveals STI concerns.

3. People boundaries
   - Allow: people both partners feel comfortable engaging with.
   - Deny: people one or both partners are not comfortable engaging with.

Then sign it — literally (e-sign, email with reply or print) or metaphorically. This isn't about legality. It's about mutual consent.

And don't forget the most important part:

Date every version. Make it easy to see how you've grown.

Event-specific agreements

"Specificity is a crucial ingredient. The more focused and particular a gathering is, the more narrowly it frames itself and the more passion it arouses."

Priya Parker, *The Art of Gathering*

Not every agreement needs to be global or permanent. Some of the most important conversations in open relating are the ones you have before specific events — especially play parties, festivals, retreats, sex clubs, and anything involving strangers, altered states, heightened sexuality, or intense sensory environments.

Event-specific agreements are like seatbelts: You hope you won't need them, but you'll be glad they're there when things get bumpy.

These agreements help you anticipate difficult moments, articulate needs before they explode, and stay connected in spaces where the energy is charged and unpredictable. They create a shared foundation so that you can relax into the experience instead of negotiating mid-trigger.

Remember: NEVER and I mean never, attempt to re-negotiate an agreement mid-scene or in front of others.

▲ Fuck Up: Yucking his yum

Evan and Max had never crafted event-specific agreements — or any agreements, really. They walked into a festival assuming they'd figure it out as they went.

On the first night, they were dancing with friends when a flirtation sparked with someone whose festival name was Butterfly. The chemistry was unmistakable. Max was buzzing with possibility. Evan felt a pang of insecurity but didn't say anything.

As the flirting heated up, Max clearly wanted to shift into play. Instead of expressing his fears or asking for reassurance, Evan blurted out, "Have sex with me first."

Max froze. He thought Evan was trying to pull him away from the scene. He declined. A fight erupted. Butterfly evaporated. The entire moment collapsed.

Evan wasn't wrong for needing reassurance. Max wasn't wrong for feeling confused. What failed them was the lack of context — no shared understanding, no emotional groundwork, no sense of how to support each other in an activated moment.

Researchers have noted that when expectations are unclear, partners in non-monogamy often interpret behavior through fear rather than reality, creating avoidable conflict. (Miller & Perlman, 2009)

Evan and Max didn't need different feelings. They needed clear event-specific agreements.

Why Event-Specific Agreements Matter

Event agreements help you clarify:

- What the experience means to you
- What you want from the night
- How much autonomy you each want
- How to reconnect when dysregulation spikes
- What behaviors are a no-go
- How you'll navigate sexual safety
- Who you are together in that space

Because when you're already overstimulated — music, lights, bodies, desire, novelty — your brain will not suddenly become better at communication.

Event agreements front-load the clarity so you can back-load the pleasure.

♥ Exercise: Craft your own event-specifics

Find a more fulsome and detailed event-specific agreements list of options at www.polyagony.com/eventagreements. Also, for a deeper, play-party-focused version of this conversation, see **Book 2: Group Play Party Dynamics**.

To avoid Max's fate, Evan could have made this request ahead of the festival. So, before attending a party or festival, sit down and discuss:

▶ How do we want to experience this event — together, separately, or fluidly?

▶ Do we want to engage with others before, after or instead of engaging with each other?

▶ Do we want hourly check-ins? Eye contact check-ins? A hand squeeze?

▶ Are there any sexual acts we reserve for each other only?

▶ Do we prefer not to play with people we just met?

▶ Do we need to leave together, or is it okay to leave separately?

▶ Are we aligned on safer-sex practices for this event? If one of us is dysregulated, how do we signal that?

Here are examples you can borrow or tweak:

"Let's check in every hour."

"Let's agree not to have penetrative sex with someone we just met tonight."

"Let's engage sexually with each other first before opening to others."

"Let's end the night together, even if we play separately."

"Let's avoid taking showers with others after scenes."

"Let's set boundaries around specific people who will be there."

And perhaps most importantly:
Talk about what each action means.

For example:

What does taking a shower with someone symbolize?

What does an overnight stay imply?

What does it mean if one of you wants to play without the other present?

Meaning, not mechanics, is where most triggers live.

Evan and Max could have avoided their meltdown if Evan had said: "Hey, if you're drawn to someone tonight, I might get insecure. I might need reassurance first, like a kiss, or two minutes of eye contact, or even just a 'You're still my person.'" It could have changed everything.

Expectations vs Reality

You can't anticipate every trigger. You're human. Your partner is human. Events are messy. Desires are surprising. Nervous systems behave badly in novel environments, and entering polyamory as a lifestyle choice will require more self reflection leading to more open communication than you might be currently accustomed to.

What you can do is prepare enough that no one gets blindsided, where needs are named, so that fears are softened, assumptions are minimized because no one has to guess your internal state, and everyone knows how to reconnect when things wobble.

You're not scripting the night. You're scaffolding the connection.

Event agreements are one of the strongest tools you have for staying in your integrity — individually and together — in spaces that push your edges.

Regular check-ins

> "Checking in allows you to address any gaps in the
> relationship before they become issues."

Dr. Nadia Teymoorian and **Dr. Martha Deiros Collado**
(KAT 103.7 FM / iHeartRadio, 2024)

One of the simplest, most underrated tools in open relating is also one of the hardest to maintain consistently: A regular check-in. Not a crisis talk. Not an argument disguised as a conversation. Not a logistical update on the carpool schedule.

A real, intentional weekly touchpoint designed to keep your relationship aligned, attuned, and emotionally connected as things change — and things will change.

In Chapter 2, we talked briefly about weekly check-ins, but this is where the practice becomes essential. Opening your relationship adds complexity, novelty, and unpredictability. A check-in gives you a place to sort through that complexity together, instead of letting it accumulate under the surface. I have been doing weekly check-ins with my partners for ten+ years. I genuinely believe it's one of the reasons my relationships are stable, even as our relationship structures evolve dramatically.

These conversations are where we realign, recalibrate, and recommit to staying connected.

What a Weekly Check-In Actually Looks Like

A good check-in isn't just "How are you?" "Good." "Cool." You want structure. Sincerity. Presence. And ideally, snacks.

Here are the five domains we cover every week:

Physical — How are our bodies? Energy? Health?

Professional — Any stress at work? Wins? Setbacks?

Financial — Anything upcoming we need to coordinate?

Sexual — Desire? Disconnection? Curiosity?

Emotional — How are we actually feeling toward each other?

We also ask: What do you need from me this week? Sometimes the answer is big. Sometimes it's tiny. Sometimes it's "Please handle bedtime twice this week." Sometimes it's "I need reassurance about your new partner."

On its own, this ritual creates trust — because neither partner is waiting for disaster to start talking.

Why It Matters More in Polyamory

In monogamy, certain conversations can drift into the background for months at a time. You often don't need to talk about jealousy, competing schedules, new attractions, or shifting emotional needs until something forces the issue. The relational ecosystem is smaller, so the pressure points surface less often.

Polyamory is different.

Everything becomes information — not because you're neurotic, but because you're navigating a larger emotional landscape. Someone catches a new crush. Someone feels anxious before a date. Someone is afraid of losing time together. Someone is riding the wave of NRE. Someone is navigating a tricky metamour relationship. Someone is feeling suddenly insecure without knowing why.

If you wait until tension hits, you're already behind. You're responding from reactivity instead of connection.

That's why regular check-ins matter so much more here. They function like emotional maintenance — tightening bolts before they shake loose, catching misunderstandings before they metastasize, and giving your relationship a place to breathe before the pressure builds.

Research on relationship satisfaction consistently shows that proactive communication — discussing needs before they become pressure points — strengthens partnership resilience.

And this is especially true in non-monogamous relationships, where complexity multiplies.

Therapists Are Not Just For Crises

> For a full directory of poly-informed therapists,
> please visit www.polyagony.com/polytherapists

If you don't already have a poly-informed therapist, it's worth finding one. Not because your relationship is falling apart. Not because anything is "wrong." But because polyamory asks you to stretch into territory most of us were never taught to navigate. A good therapist gives you tools for that journey long before you're scrambling for them.

They offer context you may not have. They give you language for feelings you've only ever felt in your body. They reflect patterns you're too close to recognize. They hold a neutral space where you can unpack fear without turning it into a fight.

Some couples use weekly therapy as their structured

check-in. Others see a therapist monthly and keep weekly conversations between themselves. There's no single right rhythm — what matters is that you're getting support, regulation, and perspective.

Because the truth is simple: your agreements will change. Your emotional needs will shift. Your comfort levels will evolve. You will both grow — in different directions, at different speeds, with different fears and different capacities.

Regular check-ins, whether supported by a therapist or held privately, make that growth something you do together, instead of something that slowly pulls you apart.

The Real Point

Agreements and check-ins are not about control.

They are about care.

They say:

"I want you to feel safe."
"I want to feel safe too."
"Let's build something we both consent to."

Opening your relationship is not just about meeting new people.

It is about building a structure strong enough to hold the love you already have.

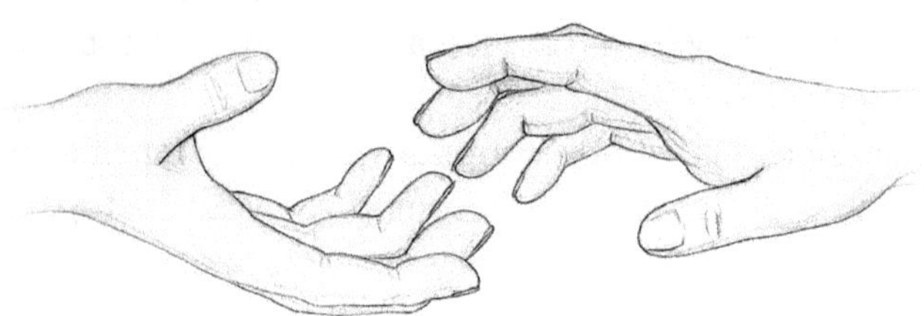

Chapter 7
Consent and Emotional Intelligence

"Consent is not the absence of 'no';
it is the presence of 'yes.'"

Jessica Valenti
(as discussed in *Yes Means Yes: Visions of Female Sexual Power and a World Without Rape*, 2008)

Consent is often talked about as if it's a simple, binary switch.
Yes or no.
Green light or red light.
Permission or refusal.

But real consent doesn't live in black and white.
It lives in tone.
In timing.
In body language.
In the nervous system.
In the subtle tension in someone's shoulders.
In the pause before a reply.
In the breath someone takes when you move closer.

Consent is not just a legal concept. And it doesn't only apply to a sexual scenario. As you negotiate agreements with your partner, consent will play a pivotal role.

It's an emotional and relational skill.

And this is where emotional intelligence enters the conversation.

You can technically get a "yes" and still miss consent entirely. You can hear the word "sure" and ignore the stiffness behind it.

You can follow all the rules and still fail to read the person in front of you.

Consent is less about scripts and more about sensitivity. Less about confidence and more about curiosity. Less about swagger and more about humility. Less about the performance of "good communication" and more about the quiet skill of paying attention.

And this is why people get it wrong — not because they're monsters, but because consent lives in subtleties most of us were never taught how to read. It's emotional. It's relational. It changes moment to moment. It asks us to hold our desire in one hand and someone else's comfort in the other, without letting either slip.

I've unknowingly violated consent before — something I'll share more about in Book 2 — and the experience changed me. It showed me how two people can walk away from the same moment with completely different interpretations. One person feels safe; the other feels pressured. One person feels connected; the other feels overwhelmed. One person believes they got a yes; the other believes they gave up a no they didn't know how to say.

There are three truths in every encounter: my truth, your truth, and whatever objective truth exists in the space between us.

Consent lives in that space — the murky middle where intention, perception, and impact collide.

To work with consent well, you can't just know your own signals. You have to learn how to read someone else's. How to adjust your pace. How to understand when enthusiasm is real and when it's borrowed from fear.

Consent is harder than people admit.

And also simpler: pay attention.

Let's look at what that actually means — not in theory, but in the body, in the room, and in the breath between two people.

Reading Consent

"When it comes to attraction, our bodies sometimes 'speak' more honestly than our words, by making subconscious, little gestures that we may not even realize."

Alison Tarlow, PsyD (quoted in *Verywell Mind*, 2024)

Consent lives in those micro-moments — the subtleties most people rush past. If you can't feel your partner, you're at high risk of assumption instead of consent. And assumption is where people get hurt.

Consent asks you to meet the person who's actually there, not the person you imagined or hoped for. It asks you to pay attention, again and again, especially in the places where desire runs hot and clarity runs thin.

Silent Consent

Silent consent is the yes someone gives because they don't want to disappoint, or don't want to rock the boat, or don't want to be replaced by someone "cooler," "freer," or "more poly" than they believe themselves to be. It's the yes offered by people who don't want to seem insecure, or needy, or jealous, or "too much." It's the yes someone gives because they've learned that caretaking is the safest way to stay loved.

It looks smooth on the surface — agreeable, flexible, easygoing — but underneath, resentment begins to gather like storm clouds. I haven't seen a major poly blow-up that didn't have one silent yes sitting somewhere at the beginning, a moment where someone abandoned themselves in the name of harmony.

That's the danger: silent consent feels peaceful in the moment, but it is peace built on self-erasure. And anything built on self-erasure eventually collapses.

The Importance of Emotional Intelligence

If you want to practice consent well, you have to learn to read what isn't spoken. Emotional intelligence isn't the bonus round in this work — it is the work. Because if you can't regulate your own system, or communicate a boundary without collapsing, or hear "not right now" without feeling rejected, it becomes nearly impossible to stay present with someone else's nervous system.

Consent asks a lot of us. It asks for self-awareness, so we know what we're bringing into a moment. It asks for regulation, so we don't make our partner responsible for calming us down. It asks for clear communication, curiosity instead of defensiveness, accountability instead of blame, and the willingness to repair when — not if — we misread the room.

And safety is the only place where real desire can actually breathe.

Check In With Yourself

"The first step of consent is tuning into your own desire, being able to feel a distinct yes or no in your system."

Adrienne Maree Brown, *Pleasure Activism* (2019)

Before you offer a yes — or interpret someone else's — it's worth pausing long enough to check which part of you is speaking. Not just your desire, but your fear. Not just your curiosity, but your attachment. Not just the thrill of the moment, but the quieter truth beneath it.

Before you escalate, before you let chemistry drag you into momentum, before you step into a dynamic that feels electric and new, ask yourself the questions most people avoid because they know the answers will change their next move.

Is this my desire — or my fear? Am I regulated, or am I pretending? Am I trying to earn love, or trying not to lose it? Am I saying yes to feel chosen, or betraying myself to stay chosen?

Your body knows the truth long before your brain catches up. Your nervous system knows even earlier. And your resentment — if you ignore yourself — will definitely know. Even if you're not in a relationship with another person, you're always in a relationship with yourself. How you treat your own yes and no becomes the template for how you'll navigate every other connection. Self-awareness is not decoration in this work; it's the root system. It's what allows you to understand your emotional responses, name your needs, and recognize when your yes is real versus when it's a mask you learned to wear to stay safe. (See Goleman, 1995) Consent isn't just something you give to others. It's something you practice with yourself first.

Practical Tip: Take 5 minutes

If something in you wobbles — even for a heartbeat — pause. Not dramatically. Not with alarm bells. Just... pause. Step out of the momentum long enough to feel yourself again.

Five minutes can save you from five weeks of confusion.

They give your nervous system a moment to settle, to breathe, to catch up with the moment. And in that pause, you can ask the questions that matter far more than "What's next?"

Do I want this? Do we want this? Is this still a yes — or has something shifted?

It's remarkable how often a tiny reset changes the entire experience. A short pause can turn a pressured yes into a grounded one, a shaky yes into a no that needed space, or a tentative moment into something more connected than either of you imagined.

Consent has never been a one-time green light. It's an ongoing state — a shared, felt sense of safety and desire that evolves as you do. Pleasure thrives when everyone is present and willing, not swept up or overwhelmed.

And because we live in a culture that is finally beginning to listen to people who name harm, the responsibility falls on all of us to slow down when something feels off. To check in before we charge ahead. To create enough space for recalibration that no one has to pretend their nervous system agrees when it doesn't.

Take five minutes. They're not a detour. They're part of the path.

The Heart of Consent

> "Consent and trust go hand in hand. To say yes to someone is also to communicate 'I trust you.'"

Donna Freitas, *Consent* (2018)

Consent shows up in the quiet places where couples forget to look. When one partner keeps pushing for "more" while the other is quietly drowning, that's a consent issue. When someone hides their needs because they're afraid of conflict, that's a consent issue. And when a partner agrees to things they're not ready for because they're terrified of losing their "woke" badge? Absolutely a consent issue.

Healthy couples understand that relational consent is just as sacred as sexual consent. They ask each other the questions that matter: What do you need to feel safe? What boundary feels important right now? How can I support your yes? How can we honor your no? And then — and this is the part most people skip — they actually listen. No debate. No defensiveness. No justifying their position or weaponizing someone's vulnerability later.

Consent inside a relationship is simply this: the ongoing agreement to treat each other's limits with care, each other's fears with softness, and each other's growth with respect.

A yes can come from fear or pressure. It can come from appeasement, insecurity, caretaking, or the quiet hope that saying yes will make someone want you.

A real yes feels different — grounded, curious, connected, free.

Consent is also contextual. It shifts with safety and pacing, with trauma history, regulation, attachment style, environment, relationship stage, emotional capacity, desire, exhaustion, even the last text your mother sent you. Consent has tides. It moves.

Consent requires self-awareness because no partner — no matter how loving — can honor boundaries you haven't learned to recognize in yourself. Your yes and your no begin with you.

Consent requires co-regulation — the willingness to slow down, to attune, to feel another body's pacing instead of imposing your own. Great lovers aren't the ones who escalate quickly. They're the ones who sense the subtle changes: your breath shortening, your posture shifting, your eyes going distant. They know the difference between leaning in and leaning away before you say a word. They don't push yellow into green or pretend red is yellow.

And consent requires repair. Not because you're careless, but because you're human. Even the most attuned lovers misread cues. What matters is how you come back.

Repair doesn't sound like defensiveness — "Why didn't you say something," "I didn't do anything wrong." That shuts the door.

Repair opens it. It sounds like: "I realize I moved too fast." "I see how that landed for you." "I wish I had checked in sooner." "Thank you for telling me."

It sounds like curiosity instead of justification. Responsibility instead of shame. A willingness to shift behavior, not just tone.

Repair means asking, "What do you need right now?" and actually listening. It means reaffirming someone's agency — their right to pause, to stop, to change direction, to feel however they feel. It means showing, not performing, that you're safe to be in connection with.

Because at its core, consent is relational. It's the promise that your desire will never outrun your care. It's the understanding that pleasure and safety aren't opposites —

they're partners. And intimacy can only go as deep as the trust beneath it.

Consent isn't meant to restrict you. It's meant to free you.

It's the foundation that allows intimacy to expand instead of overwhelm, to become erotic instead of confusing, liberating instead of destabilizing. When you practice consent with your whole self — head, heart, and body — intimacy stops being a gamble and starts becoming a place where you can actually rest.

A real yes opens a door. A real yes builds a world. And the world you build with consent is one where everyone gets to stay whole.

♥ Exercise: Green / Yellow / Red Light Consent Cues

See a more detailed explanation of the Green/Yellow/ Red Consent Cues at www.polyagony.com/consentcues.

A quick field guide for people who want to be better lovers and partners. These are not universal rules — they're cues that should prompt curiosity, slowing down, or stopping.

Green Lights

Observable cues that often signal genuine enthusiasm and embodied yes:

- Leaning in (physically, emotionally)
- Smooth, relaxed breathing
- Consistent eye contact

- Mirroring your energy or pace
- Initiating touch or closeness
- Asking questions like "Can we...?" or "I want..."
- Verbal enthusiasm ("Yes," "More," "I love this") in a grounded tone

Green lights = go, with continued attention.

Yellow Lights

Cues that require slowing down, checking in, and shifting the dynamic:

- Inconsistent pacing (lean in, lean out, lean in)
- Nervous laughter
- Freeze or stillness
- Rigid posture
- Delayed or reluctant responses
- Deflection ("Whatever you want," "I'm fine")
- Sudden quietness
- Asking for reassurance repeatedly

Yellow lights = pause, get curious, check in.

Red Lights

Cues that mean stop immediately:

- Freezing or shutting down
- Pushing your hand away
- Turning their face or body from you
- Tears, withdrawal, or distress
- Saying "I don't know," "I'm not sure," or "I guess"

- Dissociation (flatness, blank eyes, monotone voice)
- Expressing fear, discomfort, or uncertainty
- Any non-response

Red lights = stop, comfort, regulate — not negotiate.

Great lovers don't try to push yellow into green, or pretend red is yellow. They respond to the actual nervous system in front of them.

The Real Point

Consent is not a box you check. It's a relationship skill you build.

It asks for:

Presence

Curiosity

Humility

Emotional awareness

Willingness to slow down

In polyamory, where multiple hearts and bodies intersect, consent is not optional.

It is the foundation of everything.

Part Three:

Your Place in the World

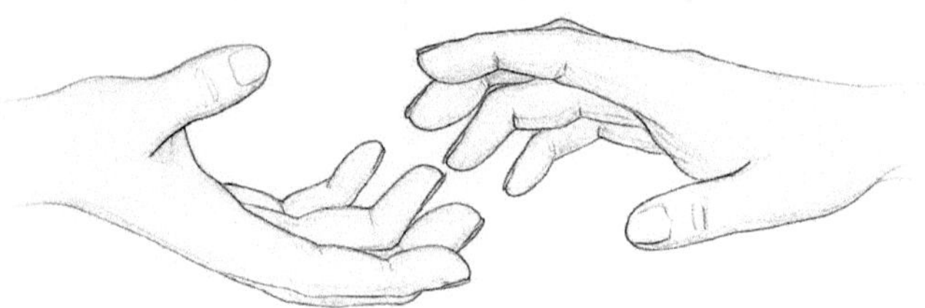

Chapter 8
Single/Solo Poly

"I believe in love, but I also believe in being single.
I can do both at the same time."

Chelsea Handler,
Life Will Be the Death of Me... and You Too! (2019)

Being single in the polyamorous world is its own adventure — sometimes exhilarating, sometimes lonely, often far more complex than people expect. I spent the first five or six years of my poly journey as a single person. I was a unicorn in the swinger scene, dating couples, building connections, and enjoying the freedom that came with not being anchored to anyone.

I loved it so much that I never imagined I'd end up partnered. I pictured having children but never pictured a father in the story. It wasn't from bitterness — it was simply the version of life that made sense to me at the time. It's important to say this out loud, because being single in non-monogamy is not inherently a transitional phase or a void waiting to be filled. It's a full and legitimate relational orientation.

But it also comes with challenges that partnered folks don't always see.

Single and solo poly are often used interchangeably, but they describe meaningfully different relationship orientations — and confusing them can create mismatched expectations for everyone involved.

Single typically describes a current relationship status. Someone may be single while practicing polyamory, open to building deeper partnerships, cohabiting, or creating shared futures when the right connection emerges. Being single and poly does not inherently reject traditional relationship structures; it simply means the person is not currently in one.

Solo poly, by contrast, is an intentional long-term relationship orientation. Solo poly people generally prioritize autonomy and self-sovereignty over traditional escalator milestones like cohabitation, marriage, or financial entanglement. They may have deeply committed, loving relationships — but they are not seeking a primary partner in the conventional sense. Neither approach is more evolved, ethical, or "correct." The key difference is intent.

If you are single, it matters to communicate whether you are open to building a primary partnership or actively not seeking one. If you are solo poly, it matters to be clear that your independence is not a placeholder, phase, or prelude to escalation.

This chapter speaks primarily to single and solo poly readers — people navigating polyamory without an anchor relationship right now, while remaining open to future structures that align with their values. If you identify as solo poly, much of this chapter will still resonate — but your long-term intentions may differ.

Much of this book focuses on primary partnerships, anchor relationships, established structures, and expanding from them. But what if you're stepping into this world without an anchor?

What if you're building a romantic ecosystem from scratch? This chapter is for you if you're navigating polyamory without an anchor relationship and want to do so with clarity and intention.

Understand Your Values

When you're single in polyamory, you become the architect of your own relationship universe. You're not negotiating from within an existing structure. You're defining your needs, your boundaries, and your desires from the ground up.

This requires clarity. And it is the best place to build an external relationship from.

Spend time understanding your values, your deal-breakers, and the agreements you hold with yourself. These will become the foundation that steadies you when emotions surge or new dynamics tempt you off your center.

▲ Fuck Up: Dating married people while seeking a primary partnership

Jeff was in his late thirties and deeply ready for a primary partner. He wanted a long-term relationship, a co-parent, someone to build a home and a life with. But dating wasn't going well, and he felt stuck.

So he did what a lot of poly people do when partnership isn't happening fast enough — he filled the space with married lovers. "It's just to pass the time," he told himself. "It's not serious."

Then he met Mia.

Mia was charming, sexy, and emotionally available in all the ways Jeff craved, except for the fact that she was in an open marriage. She told Jeff she loved him — perhaps without mentioning that to her husband — and they began seeing each other frequently. Jeff fell harder than he expected.

Then one day, her husband discovered the emotional depth of the relationship and called a veto. Overnight, Mia was gone.

Jeff was shattered. It had felt real because, for him, it was real.

Nearly a year later, he was still reeling from the heartbreak, the confusion, and the sense of betrayal. Only then did he realize that he had accidentally treated a married partner as a primary candidate — and that she had never been in a position to offer that role in return.

Being single doesn't mean you have to avoid couples entirely. But if you're seeking a primary partner, be honest with yourself about where that partner is likely (and unlikely) to come from. Otherwise, you're setting yourself up for heartbreak, resentment, and dramatic exits — sometimes all three.

The flip side? Clear communication saves everyone.

A recent lover of mine did this perfectly. When I told him I felt excited about him, he gently said, "I'm looking for a life partner. I only have capacity to be your lover-friend." His clarity made everything easier. It set the expectation from the beginning and created a foundation for a light and joyful connection — not confusion.

♥ Exercise: Know Your Relationship Foundations

To see real-life examples of relationship foundation readouts, visit www.polyagony.com/foundations.

Before dating others, define your core values, and write them down:

My Relationship Needs
Values (examples):
- Honesty
- Openness
- Generosity
- Communication
- Responsibility
- Family
- Freedom

What I Need in a Lover
Examples:
- I need a commitment to repair when ruptures occur.
- I need open communication, even when things are hard.
- I need a partner who seeks to understand, not assume.
- I need someone committed to personal and relational growth.
- I need them to respect and engage with my community.
- I need someone striving toward the highest version of themselves.

What I Won't Tolerate
Examples:
- Lying or deceit
- Exploiting others
- Taking without reciprocation
- Emotional harm
- Intentional physical harm
- Ghosting
- Treating me as an afterthought

Naming these things isn't a one-time task — it's a living document. As you date, grow, and learn more about yourself, revisit and revise your values so they stay aligned with who you are becoming.

Navigating the Hierarchy

"The greatest danger in times of turbulence is not the turbulence; it is to act with yesterday's logic."

Peter Drucker,
Management: Tasks, Responsibilities, Practices (1974)

Here's the truth: Most single poly people eventually collide with hierarchy.

For couples transitioning from monogamy into poly, hierarchy is often the training wheels, the safety net, the scaffolding that holds everything together during the early turbulence. There's nothing inherently wrong with that — but if you're single and dating couples, hierarchy becomes something you need to understand, name, and negotiate. And sometimes, it becomes something you need to avoid entirely.

▲ Fuck Up: The bait and switch break-up

Camile began dating Brit and Seb, who were new to non-monogamy. The chemistry with Seb was strong, and Camile found herself falling for him more quickly than she fell for Brit.

That's when things got weird.

Whenever she tried to make plans with Seb, Brit started appearing everywhere. If she sent Seb a sweet text, she'd get a group text back reminding her to include Brit. One night, she arrived at a scheduled date with Seb... only to find Brit waiting for her with drinks, acting like this was the plan all along.

Camile felt cornered and confused. It was the relational equivalent of a bait-and-switch.

When she finally addressed it — kindly, honestly — they both broke up with her, saying she was "disrupting their balance." In reality, she had simply named the imbalance that already existed.

Hierarchy isn't inherently bad, but unacknowledged hierarchy — especially from couples new to non-monogamy — creates confusion, resentment, and emotional whiplash for the single partner.

Understanding primary and secondary roles early, and being

brutally honest about them, helps prevent these relational blind spots.

♥ Exercise: Questions to ask when dating a couple

To see a recorded example of a couple interview,
visit www.polyagony.com/couplequestions.

Before getting too attached, ask the couple you are dating the following:

- Can I date you separately?
- How do you examine and unpack couple privilege?
- When will your partnership take precedence over my needs?
- Do I get to ask for time or attention?
- What if I fall in love with one of you but not the other?
- Do either of you have veto power?
- Will I be "out" with you publicly?
- Is there a future where I'm part of your household?

These aren't demands — they're requests for clarity.

Clarity protects everyone's heart.

Control Disparity

Many single poly people — especially when dating couples — experience control disparity. It's not always intentional, but it's common. Research indicates that among the 16% of adults who identify as non-monogamous in the U.S., at least

90% of couples use some form of hierarchy. (For statistics on non-monogamy prevalence and hierarchy in non-monogamy couples, see resources and compiled research at: https://polyagony.com/resources.)

That means the couple's relationship almost always has built-in leverage that the single person doesn't share.

Singles in these dynamics often describe feeling secondary or overlooked, like their needs come after the needs of the couple. They might notice that plans get cancelled at the last minute because the couple just got crunchy. They might feel subtly deprioritized, unsure when they're genuinely wanted versus when they're filling a gap. They might even feel like an accessory rather than a full partner — present, but not fully considered.

Camile wasn't wrong for wanting clearer structure. Jeff wasn't wrong for wanting a life partner.

The problem wasn't that they were "too needy" or "too sensitive" — the problem was misalignment and unspoken power dynamics.

▲ Fuck Ups involving Control Disparity

Couples: this part is especially for you.

Control disparity rarely shows up as one dramatic incident; it usually arrives in small, repeated moments that accumulate over time. A couple cancels a date with a single partner at the last minute because "something came up between us," leaving the single person feeling like an optional add-on rather than someone whose time deserves the same respect. Or what was supposed to be a private date with one partner slowly morphs into a couple's processing session, with the single person suddenly drafted into the role of emotional mediator. Then there are the unspoken agreements — the boundaries that exist between the couple but are never communicated to the single — which means that when an agreement gets "broken," the person on the outside ends up absorbing the fallout of expectations they never had the chance to consent to.

None of this makes singles fragile. It simply reveals how much power a couple often holds by default: social power, emotional power, scheduling power, sometimes even financial power. That doesn't make couples villains. It means they need to be exceptionally clear about their boundaries, their needs, and their limitations — not just with each other, but with anyone they choose to date. And singles have their own responsibility here too: to negotiate from clarity rather than hope, and to root their choices in self-awareness, not fantasy.

Clarifying Desire and Discernment

One of the most protective things you can do as a single poly person is get honest — first with yourself, and then with the people you're dating — about what you actually want. That might sound obvious, but in practice it's where many people get hurt.

Dating "for fun" feels very different from dating for emotional connection, long-term partnership, or co-parenting. Wanting sex without escalation is not the same as being open to building a life with someone. These differences aren't small, and they aren't implied just because you're both non-monogamous.

Clarity means being able to name what you're seeking right now, even if that answer might change later. It also means recognizing when someone else's availability — emotional, relational, or logistical — doesn't match what you're hoping for, even if you wish it did. No amount of chemistry can turn someone into a partner they are not equipped to be.

As you form new connections, discernment becomes just as important as desire. Pay attention to how people handle conflict, accountability, and communication. Notice whether you feel genuinely chosen or subtly managed. Ask yourself whether their version of polyamory aligns with yours, or whether you're already negotiating against your own needs to stay connected.

Being single poly often requires holding multiple truths at once: enjoying your independence while remaining open to connection, honoring your desires without demanding futures others haven't offered, and trusting yourself enough to walk away from dynamics that don't feel steady.

Clarity isn't about being rigid or having everything figured out. It's about protecting your nervous system and your heart by staying anchored in what you value — and allowing relationships to grow from mutual intention rather than unspoken hope.

♥ Exercise: Clarifying Desire and Discernment

To take an interactive desire quiz,
visit www.polyagony.com/desire.

Take a moment to reflect on what you are genuinely open to right now — not what you think you should want, and not what would make dating easier.

Consider the following questions, and answer them honestly for yourself:

▶ What kind of connection am I seeking at this stage of my life (play, emotional intimacy, partnership, stability, exploration, or something else)?

▶ Am I enjoying being single right now, or am I hoping this phase ends soon?

▶ If I'm dating someone who is already partnered, what expectations am I carrying — spoken or unspoken?

▶ How do I want to relate to their other partners, if at all?

▶ How do I tend to express needs or concerns when dynamics start to shift?

▶ What values or boundaries am I not willing to negotiate?

▶ What would help me stay connected without abandoning myself?

Returning to these questions periodically can help you notice when a relationship is growing in a direction that supports you, and when it's quietly pulling you off-center.

Seeking a Primary Partner

> "The first secret of getting what you want
> is knowing what you want."

Arthur D. Hlavaty

If you're looking for a primary partner, say so early. It may end some relationships, but it will save you months — or years — of painful misalignment. I've had lovers who told me upfront that they were seeking a primary, and that clarity made all the difference. Sometimes it meant parting with tenderness. Other times it meant leaning in with more intention. But honesty always made the path smoother.

Finding a primary partner in polyamory can feel impossibly hard. The dating pool is different. The expectations are different. The emotional calculus is different.

Before getting married, I remember journaling:

> "When I date single men, they try to lock me down. When I date couples, the woman thinks I'm trying to steal her man. It always ends. Why is this so hard?"

Ironically — almost comically — I wrote that the night before I met my life partner. I wasn't looking for a primary partnership. In fact, I was convinced that monogamy wasn't for me, and I didn't believe I could or should fit into a traditional structure. And yet, the connection was strong enough to build something different than anything I'd imagined.

We fell fast and hard. Living 3,000 miles apart, we found a way to spend every weekend together. And then, 90 days in, he proposed. That was eleven years ago.

That's the thing about seeking — or finding — a primary partner:

You don't get to dictate the timeline.
You don't get to script the form.
You don't get to control how it arrives.

All you can do is stay honest, stay open, and stay aligned with your values.

Primary partnership can emerge through intention or it can ambush you in the middle of a "just for fun" Tinder hookup. Both paths are valid. Both are real. Both require clarity, communication, and courage.

So trust the process — even when it feels winding, inconvenient, unpredictable, or brutally unfair. The right people show up when you're living in alignment, not when you're forcing a timeline.

Your heart matters. Your needs matter. Your insecurities matter. Your desires matter. Lean on your friends, your lovers, your polycule, your chosen family. Being single in polyamory is rich, messy, complicated terrain — but with curiosity, clarity, and honest communication, it can also become one of the most transformative chapters of your life.

Chapter 9
Considerations for Poly Parents

Polyamory on its own is a full-contact emotional sport. Polyamory with kids adds an entirely different layer of responsibility, scheduling, emotional logistics, and long-term thinking. Before you swipe right, send a flirty text, or say yes to a weekend away, you owe yourself a brutally honest question:

> How does my desire for new relationships exist
> alongside my responsibilities as a parent?

Children aren't an add-on to a polyamorous life. They are a structuring reality — one that deserves forethought, clarity, and compassion.

Research consistently shows that children thrive most when they experience emotional safety, predictable routines, and attuned caregivers. (Lamb, 2010; Bowlby, 1988) Poly parents are absolutely capable of creating those environments — it simply requires intentionality.

Entering polyamory when you or a partner has children introduces unique dynamics that deserve attention. The excitement of new relationships is real, but so is the impact on your family system. This chapter explores the considerations that help poly parents build love expansively without compromising the stability their children depend on.

Self-Reflection on Parenting Responsibilities

Before diving deeper into polyamory, take time for honest self-reflection about your parenting obligations. Children require significant time, emotional investment, and presence.

♥ Exercise: Parenting diagnostic

Find a more detailed parenting diagnostic at
www.polyagony.com/parenting.

Take a moment to ask yourself:

▶ How will new relationships fit into your family structure?

▶ How will you balance parenting duties with the needs and desires of multiple partners?

▶ What does your actual capacity — not your idealized capacity — look like?

If you have a co-parent, consider how they may feel about your exploration into polyamory. These conversations help everyone stay aligned and prevent surprises that strain family dynamics.

Studies on parental involvement underscore the importance of consistent presence in children's emotional and social development. (M.E. Lamb 2012: *Maternal and Paternal Involvement in Child Development*) Polyamory doesn't change that truth; if anything, it makes clarity even more essential.

Assessing Time and Emotional Investment

Polyamorous relationships take time — dates, conversations, aftercare, emotional processing, logistics. Parenting takes time too. If you try to pretend the hours multiply magically, something (or someone) will pay the price.

▲ Fuck Up: Getting swept away

Isla fell into a whirlwind long-distance relationship — magnetic, intoxicating, fast. She found herself flying out every two weeks to meet her new partner, stacking those trips on top of work travel. Her three children eventually said what her calendar already knew: "Trips, trips, TRIPS. You are taking too many trips."

After being gone 18 days in one month, Isla finally heard them. Her kids were naming an unmet need.

Poly life is not lived in a vacuum.

Check in with your children about how much time away feels okay — and how much feels like too much. Create agreements with them in developmentally appropriate ways, just as you do with romantic partners. Their needs deserve equal weight.

Also check in with yourself. Parenting is emotionally demanding. Adding multiple relationships amplifies that load. Make sure you have the support systems — friends, family, partners, community — that help you stay grounded rather than depleted.

Being clear about your capacity isn't just kindness to yourself and your children. It's honesty your partners need as well.

Navigating Jealousy and Insecurity

Children, like adults, notice shifts in attention and affection. Jealousy, insecurity, or clinginess are natural reactions when their world feels like it's changing.

Create space for open conversations. Let them name their feelings without correcting or dismissing them. Reassure them of your love, your consistency, and the stability of their home. If needed, seek support from a family therapist who understands polyamorous dynamics.

Research indicates that children thrive when their emotional needs are met and when they feel secure in their attachments. (Shonkoff & Phillips, 2000; Bowlby, 1988; Siegel & Bryson, 2012) The more proactively you address their feelings, the less destabilizing polyamory becomes to the family system.

Disclosing to Children

Every family will make its own decisions about what to disclose, when, and how (See Book 2 on Coming Out). Your approach may shift based on:

- age and developmental readiness
- your level of outness in the world
- risks of stigma or retaliation if a child shares information outside the home
- how involved partners will be in family life

These choices are deeply personal. There is no universal rule.

If you do plan to be open about having multiple loving relationships, the key is to do so in a way that respects your child's autonomy, privacy, and psychological safety. Not everything needs to be shared. And nothing should be sexualized or emotionally burdensome for them.

Establishing Boundaries and Agreements

Polyamorous parenting isn't just about managing your romantic life — it's about managing family ecosystems.

Just as in any relationship, establishing clear boundaries and agreements is key in polyamorous parenting, both with potential partners as well as with your children. It is important to discuss with your new partners what roles they will play in your child's life, if any, and set expectations for interactions. It is also important to craft agreements with your children so that your polyamorous life impacts them on their terms. This can help prevent misunderstandings and ensure that both your partners and your child feel secure in their environment.

First, consider creating agreements that include both partners and children (if age appropriate) regarding comfortability in how much involvement a new partner can have in family activities or how and when they will meet your children.

Second, set specific agreements with your children regarding how transparent they want you to be, what level of disclosure they are comfortable with (i.e. mom is going out with a friend tonight v. mom has a date and won't be home until tomorrow). If you have multiple children, expect that each child may have slightly different preferences, and each preference should be honored. When in doubt, err on the side of presenting less details, particularly when of a sexual or complex relationship flavor. Even if your child is curious, it is important to think about what information is developmentally appropriate for them to hear.

As you navigate these waters, consider the following:

<u>Transparency v. Age Appropriate Disclosure</u>: Be open with your children about your relationships in an age-appropriate manner. This helps them understand the dynamics without feeling excluded. At the same time, be aware of the types of information you are sharing, and avoid information that is sexual or complex in nature.

<u>Flexibility</u>: Relationships can change, and so can your family dynamics. Be prepared to revisit and adjust agreements as needed.

<u>Quality Time</u>: Make an effort to carve out special time for your children, ensuring they know they remain your priority amidst your romantic pursuits.

This probably goes without saying, but I'll say it anyway: most kids, regardless of their parents' relationship style, have zero desire to hear about their parents' sex lives.

▲ Fuck Up: Uh-Oh, Lock it Up!

Martin and his spouse Jem had recently opened their marriage and were each dating new people. They hadn't talked to their children about polyamory yet — they wanted more clarity and stability before sharing anything.

One night, Martin's nine-year-old daughter grabbed his phone to play a game and saw intimate messages and photos exchanged with his new boyfriend, Adam.

The fallout was swift and painful. The children panicked, believing the marriage was ending. They felt blindsided and unsafe. And because secrecy was tied to Adam, distrust toward him solidified before he ever had a chance to connect with them.

This situation wasn't about phone privacy. It was about preparation.

If you aren't ready to disclose certain parts of your romantic life, take appropriate precautions — phone privacy, calendars, private conversations, sex toys stored intentionally. Not because polyamory is shameful, but because children deserve clarity and containment.

Polyamory becomes destabilizing for children when secrecy replaces preparation and clarity. (Siegel & Bryson 2012)

♥ **Exercise: Take a poly parenting inventory**

Take a more detailed and up-to-date parenting inventory quiz with scoring and recommendations at www.polyagony.com/parentinginventory.

Take a moment to reflect on your current family dynamics

and how they might be impacted by polyamory. Use these prompts in a journal, a conversation with a partner, or a quiet moment alone.

Current Dynamics

▶ Describe your current family structure. Who are the key players (e.g., children, co-parents, etc.)?

▶ How do you currently allocate your time between parenting and personal relationships?

Impact of Polyamory

▶ How do you imagine adding new romantic relationships will change your family dynamics?

▶ What concerns do you have about how this might affect your children?

Balancing Responsibilities

▶ What strategies can you implement to ensure that your parenting responsibilities remain a priority?

▶ How can you create a schedule that accommodates both your romantic life and your role as a parent?

Communication

▶ How can you initiate conversations with your children about your exploration into polyamory? What key points would you want to convey?

▶ Are there any specific fears or concerns you think your children might have? How can you address these proactively?

Support Systems

▶ Identify the support systems you currently have in place (friends, family, community groups). How can these be leveraged as you navigate polyamory?

▶ Are there any additional resources or communities you would like to explore to gain support?

Building a Supportive Community

Finding other poly parents — through local meetups, online forums, social groups, conferences — can provide tremendous grounding for both you and your kids. These communities offer:

shared wisdom

normalization

emotional support

resources for difficult conversations

They also give your children peers who understand non-traditional family structures. That sense of belonging can reduce feelings of isolation or "being different." (E. Sheff, ***The Polyamorists Next Door***, 2014)

Navigating polyamory as a parent is a multifaceted journey. It requires intentionality, strong communication, realistic time management, and an unwavering commitment to your children's emotional well-being.

When done thoughtfully, your romantic life and your

parenting life don't compete — they coexist. They inform each other. They grow each other. And they show your children, through lived example, that love is abundant, flexible, honest, and human.

Your primary responsibility is to ensure your children feel loved, secure, and understood as you explore who you are becoming.

Conclusion: Is it worth it in the end?

This is such an interesting question. I've been asking everyone I interview, and I've spoken to more than a hundred people—individuals from various walks of life, different socioeconomic statuses, and diverse poly structures. I've talked to people who have transitioned from poly to monogamous relationships, monogamous to poly, and everything in between. I've interviewed those in "don't ask, don't tell" marriages, solo poly individuals, parallel poly folks, and relationship anarchists.

As I've engaged with these diverse perspectives, I've asked repeatedly, "Is it worth it? Is it worth it in the end?"

The responses vary. Not everyone says yes. Not everyone is committed to remaining poly for the rest of their lives. Many are open to evolving in new and different directions. Yet, there remains a resounding sentiment: "It's worth it for me to have gone through this experience. It's worth it for me to have taken on this journey of self-discovery."

I've experienced significant trauma over the past five years.

I had a second child at 22 weeks, August, who lived only four days. The loss was devastating, both emotionally and physically, as I navigated the trauma my body endured during that time. When my family felt ready, we pursued adoption.

Shortly thereafter, a friend of mine murdered his wife—with whom he had three children under the age of six. After the tragedy, each attorney representing the three boys reached out to me (having heard that we were seeking adoption), asking my family to fight for custody. So, we did. We fought for those children because they deserved to have someone to advocate for their best interests.

In court, our lifestyle and poly identity were put on trial. We were interrogated about how our choices could affect our children and our relationship. Our adoption agency faced scrutiny regarding our poly decisions. Ultimately, the judge ruled against us, stating that we needed to reconsider our life choices because we were poly. Following this, the adoption fell through—an incredibly painful experience.

In response to such circumstances, there are two primary paths one can take. One way is to revert to monogamy, to seek comfort in what society deems acceptable, prioritizing the vision of parenthood over a lifestyle choice. I don't blame anyone for choosing this path; it's a completely defensible viewpoint.

The other path is to stand firm in the face of persecution for loving others openly, the path I ultimately chose. I feel compelled to advocate for what I believe is right—for myself and for countless others - for a life where we can love without filters, embrace one another, build community, and choose unconventional paths.

This stance can be threatening to others. As I've come out of the closet over the past months while writing this book, I've faced numerous judgments—from family members, parents, and even acquaintances who've come out of the woodwork to express that "God is frowning on your life path."

I've received articles claiming that polyamory is merely the latest fad of the ruling class—ironic, considering that many of these articles are behind paywalls. I've been told that it's impossible to be both authentic and public.

Yet, I cannot be any other way. This is who I am.

This is the shape of my heart: I am a bisexual, queer, polyamorous woman, deeply in love with my family, committed to living in California, and striving to be a fully present mother on Cape Cod.

It's incredibly hard and confusing. My lovers come from all walks of life—rich and poor, tall and short, young and old, extroverted and introverted. They are all beautifully human and deserving of my love. I love them. I love you. I love. I will fight for love until the day I die.

Whether you choose this path or another, I encourage you to love—yourself, others, and to love with abandon. Embrace the uncomfortable aspects of your identity because the world deserves to see the real you. All of you.

As a mother first and foremost, I will support my child in whatever he chooses. If he identifies as transgender, non-binary, or loves anyone—men, women, or anyone in between—I will support him. Whether he chooses to be loud or quiet, public or private, or live anywhere in the world, he will have my unwavering support.

That's the world I'm committed to building—a world where my child and others can thrive. I believe you share this commitment, too, because you're reading this book. Thank you from the bottom of my heart for standing for humanity. We can only create this world together.

What Comes Next

You've built the foundation. You know yourself — your why, your blueprint, your communication style, your attachment patterns. You've built agreements with your partner. You've decided how you'll walk in the world.

This is just the beginning.

In *Polyagony: The Expansion*, we'll explore what happens when others enter — the joys and challenges of being a hinge, navigating metamour relationships, group dynamics, play parties, aftercare and coming out to your friends and the world. That book is for when you're ready to add complexity to what you've built here.

And in *Polyagony: The Reckoning*, we'll face the hardest parts — when the papercuts accumulate, when agreements break, when relationships need to end or transform. That book will be there when you need it.

For now, stand on the ground you've built.

You're ready.

About the Author

Candace Klein is a lawyer, entrepreneur, and transformational leader whose work spans finance, technology, and human development. Born in Cincinnati, Ohio, she graduated from the Salmon P. Chase College of Law and practiced law before founding and leading mission-driven companies. She served as CEO of several companies and has held senior executive roles large corporations and startups. Today, she facilitates emotional intelligence and transformational workshops in San Diego and Cape Cod. She also co-authored *Typhoon Honey: The Only Way Out Is Through* on emotional growth.

Contact her at
www.polyagony.com

VITALITY

growing love,
sharing holistic self-care,
and inspiring creative expression.

We invite you to explore with us through our
affordable, friendly drop-in classes...
in person & online

vitalitycincinnati.org

and our books

vitalitybuzz.org